D0675301

How Koreans Talk

How Koreans Talk

A Collection of Expressions

Sang-Hun Choe
Christopher Torchia

Unhengnamu

FOREWORD

"You can repay a debt of a thousand gold coins with a single nice word," a Korean proverb says.

Koreans draw on proverbs and slang to scoff, praise or just get a point across. Some exclaim "That's the carrot!" when they agree with you. If things don't work out, they grumble about "eating water." Anger them, and they growl: "You die! I die!" But they also advise caution, saying: "Don't touch your hat in the pear orchard."

Korean talk is populated by puppies, tigers, frogs, ticks, persimmons, rice cakes, empty cans, fluorescent lights and military advisers.

This book is a collection of expressions, along with comments on their origin, and excursions into Korean history, folk tales and contemporary culture. It leaves out many idioms, but aspires to reflect part of the Korean character through the humor and imagery of language.

Some expressions are used mainly by older people. There is also slang that is popular only among the young.

A lot of terms in this book illustrate the gritty side of Koreans, who have endured conflict and hardship. A handful of expressions are improper in a formal Korean setting, but they were included for their historical and cultural background.

CONTENTS

1
Eat, Eat: Rice Is Everything

Never free from the threat of hunger,
traditional Korea generated many phrases that
dwell on food.

001 》 Have you eaten yet?

Siksahaeteoyo? 식사했어요?

A casual greeting that dates from an era of war and famine. Hunger was widespread in South Korea until the 1960s, and still is in North Korea. In the South, a man who asks the question isn't necessarily offering to take you out for lunch. Defectors from North Korea say the phrase is not a popular greeting in their country.

A common greeting in South and North Korea is, "Were you safe overnight?" (*bamsae byeolgo eopseuseyo?*) The expression is also believed to have originated in a time when bad things happened overnight: bandit raids, guerrilla attacks and death from hunger and disease.

Guksu eonje meokji? 국수 언제 먹지?

002 》 When will I have a chance to eat your noodles?

When are you getting married? Noodles are a common dish at wedding banquets. Long noodles symbolize longevity, and are popular at celebrations such as the birthdays of parents.

003 》 I ate water!

Mulmeokeotda! 물먹었다!

I lost out. An office worker says this after missing a promotion or a party. So does a journalist who was scooped. The saying implies that the loser only got to drink water while others had a hearty meal.

Sikeunjuk meogi 식은죽 먹기

004 》 It's like slurping cold porridge.

It's a piece of cake. Also: "That's as easy as eating rice cake while lying down" (*nuweseo tteokmeogi*).

Geumgangsando sikhugyeong 금강산도 식후경

005 》 You should eat even before sightseeing at Diamond Mountain.

Eat first, no matter what temptation or chore awaits. People often say this when they mean: "Let's stop work for a bit and eat."

From ancient times, Koreans have flocked to Diamond Mountain, and its beauty has inspired poets, singers and artists. The mountain is in the southeastern corner of North Korea.

Koreans used this expression well before 1945, when their peninsula was divided in two. For North Korea, Diamond Mountain turned out to be as precious as its name- sake. The country opened the mountain to South Korean tourists in 1998 and earned hundreds of millions of dollars in desperately needed hard currency. The venture became a symbol of South Korea's "sunshine" policy of trying to pry open North Korea through economic and other exchanges, but it ran into trouble because not enough tourists signed up for the trip.

Meokgo jukeun gwisinyi ttaekkali jotda 먹고 죽은 귀신이 때깔이 좋다

006 » Not all corpses look the same; the person who died while eating looks healthier.

Whatever the situation, you've got to eat. Farmers consume huge amounts of rice at one sitting because it is their main source of energy for a day of toil in the fields. Famines were frequent a long time ago, and a rotund belly was a status symbol, a sign of wealth and authority.

Bap meokyeo juna! 밥 먹여 주나!

007 » It won't fill me up with rice!

Let's be practical! Koreans say this when opposing an idea or project that won't do them any good.

Jukdo anigo bapdo anigo 죽도 아니고 밥도 아니고

008 » It's neither rice nor porridge.

A gray area, somewhere in between. A big project that goes nowhere. Cook rice with a lot of water, and you end up with porridge. An unskilled cook turns rice kernels into a mush that's neither rice nor porridge.

Kkamagwi gogi meokeotna? 까마귀 고기 먹었나?

009 » Did you eat crow meat?

Can't you remember anything? The origin of this phrase lies in a fable. The king of the underworld ordered his emissary, the crow, to deliver a letter to the lieutenants who shepherded humans into the depths. As it flew, the crow saw a dead, decaying horse. It circled over the carrion, torn between its duty as messenger and the temptation of a feast. The crow succumbed and picked the carcass clean. When it came to its senses, it discovered that the letter was gone, swept away by the wind. Fearing punishment, the flustered bird told the king's lieutenants that they were supposed to escort as many people as possible to hell. Wailing filled villages as the innocent died mysteriously and were herded into the underworld. Humans have loathed the crow ever since, branding it a forgetful bird and an augury of death. Some rural Koreans spit three times when they hear a crow, believing the ritual will repel the bad omen.

Gichahwatongeul salmameokeotna 기차화통을 삶아 먹었나?

010» Did you boil and eat the locomotive's smokestack?

You sound like a foghorn. Locomotives arrived in Korea in the early 20th century, and some Koreans believed the monstrous machine's whistle and puffing came from the smokestack, rather than the driver's cabin and engine.

RICE

An Asian staple for centuries, rice is consumed at virtually every meal in Korea. Consumption is decreasing because economic prosperity and trade with other countries have made meat and other alternatives more available. A Korean who says, "Let's go have rice" (*bapmeokeureogaja*), is suggesting that you have a meal together, but the menu doesn't have to include rice.

A generation ago, rice was everywhere. Koreans ate rice cake (*tteok*) and drank rice wine (*takju*). Children ate candies and syrups made of rice (*yeot*). Rice was the main food offering in ancestral rites. People used rice husks as padding for pillows. Roofs were built with rice straw, which made the Korean hut a fire hazard. Villagers burned straw to cook food or warm their rooms and mixed it with animal droppings to make compost.

Walls and floors were mud mixed with rice straw. People wove straw bags (*gamani*) and straw mats (*meongseok*). Straw bags were such an essential means of storage and transportation that they were collected as taxes. People used them to carry rice and other grains. They filled them with sand and gravel and stacked them to build levees. Straw mats served as carpets for ordinary folk.

"She refused to dance when the straw mat was rolled out." She had been ready to perform or tackle a task but backed off because the cheers of others unnerved her.

Villagers rolled a villain into a straw mat and pummeled him. The victim couldn't tell who the assailants were, so those delivering the blows were less tentative.

For years, South Korea protected its rice market, providing cheap loans for rice farmers and buying large amounts of rice to boost domestic rice prices. But under a 1994 global free trade agreement, the country began opening its market to cheaper foreign rice. Farmers staged violent protests, complaining that imports would destroy their livelihood. They carried banners with an old slogan of the Yi Dynasty: "Farmers are the foundation of the world!" (*nongsa cheonhajidaebon*).

Tteok jul sarameun saenggakdo anneunde kimchigukbuteo masinda 떡 줄 사람은 생각도 않는데, 김칫국부터 마신다

011 » Don't drink kimchi soup before somebody offers you rice cake.

Don't jump the gun. Korea's trademark dish, kimchi, is a spicy sauerkraut made from cabbage, turnips or virtually any other vegetable. It's as much a staple as rice. Koreans used to eat rice cake and wash it down with kimchi soup. So you're jumbling the natural order of things if you eat the soup first.

Namui tteoki keoboinda 남의 떡이 커보인다

012 » The other man's rice cake always looks bigger.

The grass always looks greener on the other side.

Bogi joheun tteokyi meogyido jotda 보기 좋은 떡이 먹기도 좋다

013 » A rice cake that looks good tastes good.

Appearances matter. But you can't judge a book by its cover, as this saying suggests: "You can't judge bean paste soup by the earthen bowl." Bean paste soup is cooked and served in an earthen bowl. The bowl is bulky and has a rough surface, but the soup is a Korean favorite.

Geurimui tteok 그림의 떡

014 » Rice cake in the picture.

You can see it, but you can't eat it. Pie in the sky.

Naneun chanbapida 나는 찬밥이다

015 » I am cold rice.

I get the cold shoulder from everybody. Rice tastes best when hot.

Ssalbap boribap garilsuitna? 쌀밥 보리밥 가릴 수 있나?

016 » I'm not in a position to choose between rice and barley.

I'll take whatever is handy. Or "I can't choose between hot and cold rice." Poor families ate barley, sometimes with potatoes. The rich ate rice. Barley took longer to cook than rice, and wasn't as tasty. Over the centuries, barley became a symbol of poverty.

Miunnom tteok hana deo junda 미운 놈 떡 하나 더 준다

017 » Give one more rice cake to a person you don't like.

If treated well, a miscreant will shape up. Some commentators say South Korea has pursued this lenient philosophy in its dealings with North Korea. Eager to promote peace and coax the North into opening up, the South has provided its neighbor with aid and other concessions in recent years. Progress is erratic despite the first-ever summit of the leaders of the two Koreas in 2000.

Duli meokdaga hanaga jukeodo moreunda 둘이 먹다가 하나 죽어도 모른다

018 » You wouldn't notice even if your friend at the same table dies.

Praise for a delicious meal.

Sintobulyi 신토불이

019 » Your body and earth are not two different things.

According to an old belief, humans come from the earth and return to it when they die. They eat plants or animals that eat those plants. Thus, after many centuries, the soil of a region is said to influence the characteristics of its inhabitants. Many Koreans believe food grown in Korea is best for Koreans and local medicinal herbs have their maximum effect on Koreans. Businesses often print *sintobulyi* on food packages to urge people to consume local products. Most Koreans favor local beef, even though it's more expensive than imports.

Songchungineun solripeul meokeoya handa 송충이는 솔잎을 먹어야 한다

020 » ## Pine caterpillars must eat pine needles.

Accept who you are and what you have. The pine is the most common tree in Korea. King Se Jo of the Yi Dynasty was visiting a Buddhist temple in Sokri Mountain in central South Korea when he saw a towering pine tree in the way. As the royal sedan approached, according to the legend, the tree lifted its branches to clear the way for the king. The grateful monarch appointed the pine tree to an honorary Cabinet post. A national treasure, the majestic tree still stands today.

Baetsoke geojiga deuleoanjatna? 뱃속에 거지가 들어앉았나?

021 » ## Is a beggar squatting in your stomach?

You eat too much, too quickly. Mothers say this to kids who eat voraciously but remain as thin as grasshoppers.

Juk ssweoseo gaejunda 죽 쒀서 개준다

022 » ## You made porridge but ended up giving it to the dog.

A waste of time and energy.

Jakeun gochuga maepda 작은 고추가 맵다

023 》 Small pepper is hotter.

Koreans think short people are gritty. If you make fun of a Korean man's diminutive stature, he might kick up dirt and charge toward you, fuming: "I will show you that a small pepper is hotter, you dumb telephone pole." Koreans point out that two of South Korea's former military rulers – Park Chung-hee and Chun Doo-hwan – were on the short side. Koreans traditionally think tall men have a sense of humor but are indecisive. They call them *singeopda*, or "lacking salt."

Pepper is an ingredient in virtually all Korean dishes. Koreans sprinkle pepper powder in their soups, chew pickled pepper, and munch green peppers dipped in red pepper paste. Kimchi cabbage laced with red pepper and garlic is an all-time favorite.

"He's sprinkling pepper powder." The man is a spoiler.

Kongeuro meju ssundahaedo an mitneunda 콩으로 메주 쑨다해도 안 믿는다

024 》 I won't believe you even if you say the meju is made of soybeans.

I will never believe you. Meju is a cone of soybean mash used to make soybean sauce. Every Korean knows meju comes from soybeans. Today, meju is mass-produced in factories. Rural families still make the stuff at home. Housewives pound steamed soybeans with a mortar and pestle. The mash is molded into truncated cones the size of rugby balls. These cones, or meju, are wrapped with rice straw and hung from the living room ceiling – a distinctive autumn scene in a rural household.

"He's got a meju head," means he has a cone-shaped head, or is a conehead.

In the winter, the cones are moved into the bedroom, where they continue to ferment, filling the room with a moldy smell. In the spring, housewives break the cones into fist-sized pieces and put them in a large earthenware jar, which is then filled with water. They add salt, whole red peppers and a few lumps of charcoal, which are said to keep insects away. The jar is left open in the sun. When a black liquid forms, it is ladled out and boiled to become soybean sauce. The remaining contents of the jar become fermented bean paste, called *doenjang*. Along with red-pepper paste, *doenjang* and soybean sauce are the most widely used condiments in Korea.

Gudeogi museoweo jang mot damgeuna 구더기 무서워 장 못 담그나

025 》 Just because you fear maggots doesn't mean you should give up making soybean sauce.

Don't let obstacles deter you. Housewives often keep the lid off the soybean paste jar to help its contents ferment in the sun. Sometimes, flies lay eggs and maggots form.

Sone jangeul jijinda 손에 장을 지진다

026 》 I'll cook bean paste soup on my palm.

I'll eat my hat. I'll bet the farm that it's not true. Or the expression can be a solemn vow to keep a promise. "If I don't do it, I'll cook...."

Ttonginji doenjanginji moreunda 똥인지 된장인지 모른다

027 》 He can't distinguish between excrement and bean paste.

He can't tell good from bad. The colors of excrement and bean paste are similar.

Dubu jjareudeutyi 두부 짜르듯이

028 》 As though cutting bean cake.

Arbitrarily. "You can't just end a relationship as though cutting bean cake."

Housewives soak soybeans in water, grind them and pour the mixture into a sieve. The milky liquid is boiled and strained through a hemp bag. The curd that remains in the bag hardens into a white bean cake. Housewives cut the cake into small cubes for cooking.

Kongnamul sirugatyi 콩나물 시루같이

029 》 Packed like bean sprouts.

Like sardines. Today, bean sprouts, an ingredient in many Korean dishes, are mass-produced by grocery suppliers. But some rural families still grow their own sprouts. A housewife spreads raw beans on a strainer made of sticks and rice straw in a jar with holes in the bottom. She places the jar on wooden bars straddling a large shallow bowl. She douses the beans with water, which collects in the large bowl beneath. Several times a day, the housewife scoops the water and pours it on the beans. Within a week, the jar is densely packed with fast-growing bean sprouts. Before greenhouses became widespread in the 1970s, virtually every household kept a bean sprout jar indoors in the winter to grow soybeans and consume the sprouts.

Bean shoots get bigger every day. A "bean sprout" is also a thin, tall kid.

Bulgasari cheol meokdeut handa 불가사리 철 먹듯 한다

030 》 He ate like Bulgasari eating metal.

He ate like a pig. Bulgasari, or "unstoppable monster," is a creature of legend. Centuries ago, toward the end of the Koryo Dynasty, a widow in the city of Songdo (what is today Kesung, in North Korea) was sewing when she saw a small beetle-shaped creature. It crawled up her leg, across her shoulder, down to her hand and onto her finger. Then it gobbled her needle.

Mesmerized, the widow picked up another needle, and the creature devoured that too. She kept the outlandish animal as a pet, feeding it spoons and hoes. The ever-expanding creature ate anything made of metal: scissors, kitchen utensils, door hinges, rakes and even the widow's bronze chamber pot. Then it went on a culinary tour of the town. Government troops tried to kill the giant monster, which looked like a bear with a tiger's head, an elephant's nose, a water buffalo's eyes, a cow's tail and a lion's paws. Spears, arrows and swords bounced off the monster's hide, and it slurped up the weapons like noodles. Soldiers hurled fireballs from catapults, but it inhaled the flames and breathed fire. Villagers called the scourge "Bulgasari."

Then a Buddhist monk with a long cane appeared. When the monster saw the monk, it tucked its tail between its legs, eyes downcast. The monk chastised the creature and whacked it on the back with his cane. The monster crumbled into a heap of metal objects – needles, spoons, spades, pots, and all the other things it had eaten. Peace returned, but the legend says that the creature's rampage contributed to the collapse of the Koryo Dynasty.

Even today, Koreans say people who engage in gratuitous violence and get away with it are "Songdo bulgasari." They're untouchables.

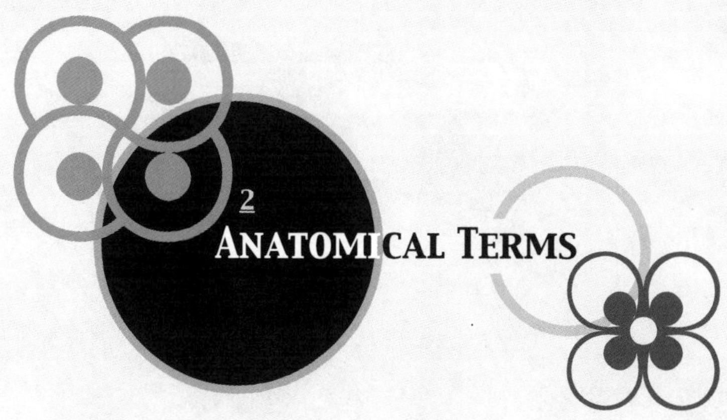

2
ANATOMICAL TERMS

From hair to feet, body parts are rich with symbolism and are common components of Korean expressions.

Meoriga pappuriga doedorok 머리가 파뿌리가 되도록

031 » Until your hair turns into leek roots.

Till death do you part. A stock phrase cited by a wedding officiator. Leek roots are white and sparse.

Nunuteum chinda 눈웃음 친다

032 » She is smiling at you with her eyes.

The come-hither look.

Nundojang jjikda/Eolguldojang jjikda 눈 도장 찍다 / 얼굴 도장 찍다

033 » I put my eye seal/stamp on it.

I'm determined to have it. Until recently, all Koreans stamped letters, documents and contracts with personal seals. They're still in use, though signatures are now widespread.

A headhunter spotting a prospect in the job market puts his "eye stamp" on the young professional. A couple stamps its "eye seal" on a new apartment. A man who jostles to meet a powerful person is trying to leave his "face stamp." People joke that they go to the wedding of their boss's daughter to leave their "face stamps" on the boss.

A slang term similar to "eye stamp" is *jjikeotda* or *jjim.* It refers literally to the act of signing with a stamp or seal. In street talk, it refers to a teen ritual: licking your thumb and stamping the fingerprint on the forehead or cheek of your lover.

It means: "Now you belong to me, and don't even think about dating anybody else."

Nune ssangsimjireul kyeogo 눈에 쌍심지를 켜고

034 » Her eyes are lit wicks.

There are daggers in her eyes.

Nae koga seokjada 내 코가 석자다

035 » My own nose is three feet long.

I've got enough problems of my own. This idiom reminds Koreans of mucus dangling from a child's nose.

Linguists believe the root of this saying was in a Shilla Dynasty yarn about Bang Yi, a poor, kind man with a rich, stingy brother. Bang Yi asked his brother to give him some silkworm eggs and grain seeds so he could farm. His spiteful brother steamed the eggs and seeds before giving them to Bang Yi, who tended them day and night without knowing they were sterile.

Only one egg hatched. But the silkworm grew as big as a bull. The envious brother killed it. Then, out of nowhere, vast numbers of silkworms squirmed to Bang Yi's house, turning him into a silkworm king.

From the steamed seeds, one sprout emerged. A bird fluttered by, plucked the sprout and glided away. Bang Yi chased the bird into the woods. He lost his way and at nightfall, he spotted goblins using a magic club to transform rocks and trees into rice cake, meat, fruit and liquor. Hours later, the drunken goblins staggered off, absentmindedly leaving their club. Bang Yi grabbed it, and soon he was a rich man.

Bang Yi's envious brother headed to the woods, determined to find a magic club for himself. By this time, though, the goblins had sobered up and were annoyed at losing their club. They captured the brother and pulled his nose into an elephant trunk three feet long before letting him loose.

Ne kona dakkara 네 코나 닦아라

036 » Go and wipe your own nose.

Mind your own business. The nose symbolizes pride, and Korean is rich with nose-related expressions.

"I broke his nose bone." I humiliated him.

"His nose is so high that it might touch the heaven." He's stuck up.

Somebody with a "hard nose bone" is stubborn and arrogant.

"I covered my nose." I was ashamed.

"They put a nose ring on me." They control me.

"She farted through her nose." She sneered.

An old name for a common cold was *goppul*, or a "nose on fire."

A flat nose is “a dog-paw nose.” A turned-up nose is a “sky-light nose.” A hooked nose is “a hawk’s beak nose.” A bulbous nose is a “fist nose.”

Koreans refer to toddlers as *koheulligae*, or “snivelers.”

They call a Westerner *kojaengyi*, or “a creature with a big nose,” or just “big nose.”

Jwi japameokeun goyangyi 쥐 잡아먹은 고양이

037 » Your lips remind me of a cat that just ate a rat.

You’re wearing too much lipstick.

Ipsuli eopeumyeon iga sirida 입술이 없으면 이가 시리다

038 » If you lose your lips, your teeth get cold.

Close partners share the same destiny. During the Cold War, China said its relationship with North Korea was “as close as lips and teeth.” The two communist countries fought together against South Korea and U.S.-led United Nations troops in the Korean War. Today, China provides aid to the impoverished and isolated North. It chose market reforms and established diplomatic ties with South Korea in 1992.

Ipyi yeolgaerado hal mali eopda 입이 열 개라도 할 말이 없다

039 » Even if I had ten mouths, I couldn't say a thing.

I was speechless with guilt.

Hyeoga kkoida 혀가 꼬이다

040 » His tongue curled up.

He was so drunk that he was difficult to understand. The phrase also applies to a Korean whose pronunciation of his native language changes after living abroad. To put on a sophisticated air, some people mimic the accent of a Korean who has spent time in the United States. Down-to-earth people hate that and say, "Stop rolling your tongue."

Motsaenggin ge joenya? 못 생긴 게 죄냐?

041 » Is it a crime to look ugly?

People, especially men, say this in jest when friends gossip about their appearance.

This one-liner was a favorite of the late Lee Joo-il, South Korea's most famous standup comedian. Popular from the early 1980s to the 1990s, Lee entertained with his comic "duck" walk and self-deprecating remarks about his looks, which audiences agreed were far from handsome. Lee had an upturned nose. In his slapstick routines, he played the role of an ugly, stammering dimwit.

When people compared Lee with authoritarian President Chun Doo-hwan because both men were balding, officials banned him from the TV screen for a year. Lee was elected to the national legislature in the 1990s and lawmakers fought to smother their laughter when he spoke in the parliament. Lee later said, "I didn't know until I joined the National Assembly that politicians were comedians."

A chain-smoker, Lee was diagnosed with lung cancer and became an anti-smoking activist before he died in 2002 at the age of 61.

042 » Clothes are your wings.

Otyi nalgaeda 옷이 날개다

People judge you by what you wear. In a folk tale, a logger saved a deer chased by hunters. The grateful deer told the logger that a group of nymphs would bathe in a secret pond by the light of the full moon, and that he should steal the clothes of one. The logger did so. After bathing, all the nymphs flew back to heaven save the one without clothes, which served as wings. The logger offered to take her back to his house, and they soon got married. The deer had told the logger that he should never tell the nymph about the theft until she had given birth to three children. After two children, the man got complacent.

"No woman would leave her husband and children," he thought.

One night, the logger told his wife about the deer and her clothes. The wife begged to wear her old dress just once, and the logger let her do so. Then, she flew away with a child under each arm.

Byeorukgando ppaemeokeul saram 벼룩간도 빼먹을 사람

043 》 He could persuade a tick to give up its liver.

He's a con-artist. "He could steal the liver from a tick and make a dish of sashimi out of it," people say about an extortionist. Or: "He patted me on the back while removing my liver to eat."

Koreans regard the liver, a symbol of courage and vitality, as the most important body part. In many legends, monsters only eat the liver of their victims.

"I thought my liver would fall out." I was startled.

Ganyi keuda/Ganyi bueotda 간이 크다 / 간이 부었다

044 》 You've got a big/swollen liver.

You've got a lot of nerve. A reckless character deserves the remark: "Your liver is so big that it's hanging outside your belly."

You can reverse the expression. A coward or somebody seized by fear has a tiny liver. "When I saw that mad dog of a teacher walking toward me, I thought my liver was shriveling to the size of a bean."

Sseulgae eoptneun saram 쓸개 없는 사람

045 » He's missing his gallbladder.

He has no pride, no mettle. The gallbladder also symbolizes courage. People who see something scary or gruesome say: "I felt a chill sweeping over my liver and gallbladder."

Gane buteotda, sseulgaee buteotda 간에 붙었다, 쓸개에 붙었다

046 » He darts between the liver and gallbladder.

He'll switch sides in a flash if it suits him.

Gomeun sseulgae ttaemune jukgo, sarameun ip ttaemune jukneunda 곰은 쓸개 때문에 죽고 사람은 입 때문에 죽는다

047 » A bear gets killed for its gallbladder; a man gets killed because of his mouth.

Watch your words. Bear gallbladders were a traditional treatment for ailments from toothache to epilepsy. Smuggled bear gallbladders are still sold illegally in some Asian countries, including South Korea, where each is worth thousands of dollars. In recent years, tightened customs inspections have curtailed smuggling of gallbladders into South Korea. But police believe the organ is still sold in tiny portions.

Biwi matchuda 비위 맞추다

048 》 Please her spleen and stomach.

Flatter somebody. "Our spleens and stomachs don't get along" means there is no chemistry between us.

When Koreans find food or somebody revolting, they say: "My spleen and stomach hurt."

Sokyi tanda 속이 탄다

049 》 My insides are burning.

I've got the jitters. If a kid gets into trouble with the law, Koreans say: "His mother must feel as if her intestines have burned up and turned into charcoal."

Another expression of maternal agony is the Chinese *dan jang*, or "intestines broken into pieces." A general was traveling through the Three Gorges of the Yangtze River when he found one of his soldiers carrying a baby monkey that he had caught in the woods. As the ship sailed along the river, the mother monkey scampered over the rugged cliffs, crying for its baby. When the ship reached its destination after a 100-mile journey, the mother monkey jumped onto the ship and collapsed before its baby. The general opened the mother's belly and found its intestines broken into pieces.

A Korean folk song, "Miari Pass of Broken Intestines," tells of the suffering of women whose sons and husbands were hauled away by retreating communist troops during the Korean

War. Most young men never returned. Women sent off their men at Miari Pass, now a commercial district in Seoul.

Male ppyeoga itda 말에 뼈가 있다

050 His words have bones.

His comments harbor hidden meaning or criticism. A similar expression: "His words bristle with thorns."

Baekkop ppajineunjul alatda/ Baekkop japgo utda 배꼽 빠지는 줄 알았다 / 배꼽 잡고 웃다

051 I laughed so hard that I thought my belly button would pop out.

People also say: "I laughed so hard that I had to hold my belly button" (for fear that it would come loose).

Baeboda baekkopyi keuda 배보다 배꼽이 더 크다

052 Her navel is bigger than her belly.

She's got her priorities mixed up.

Bulal ttego janggaganda 불알 떼고 장가간다

053 He left his testicles behind when he went to his wedding.

He devoted a lot of time to something, but neglected the heart of the matter. For example, a guy went to a concert but left his ticket at home.

Jukeun adeul bulal manjigi 죽은 아들 불알 만지기

054 » Touching the balls of a dead boy.

A useless gesture. Grandparents often fondled their infant grandson, cooing, "My boy, let me touch your balls." The common gesture was a show of affection.

Mijual gojual kaeda 미주알 고주알 캐다

055 » He is digging into my rectum.

A nosy parker. *Mijual*, an old term for the rectum, survives only in this popular phrase. *Gojual* has no meaning, but adds rhythm.

056 » She's wagging her tail.

Kkori chinda 꼬리친다

She is a flirt. In legends, the combination of a woman and tail unsettles male folk. The nine-tailed fox is a folk tale villain. Disguised as a beautiful woman, the fox tries to entrap and kill a man and eat his liver, thereby securing a tenth tail and becoming a human being. The lore usually features a hero who stymies the conniving creature.

Modern men describe a temptress as a "nine-tailed fox." *Bulyeou*, or "a flaming fox," is a female knave.

Kkoriga gilmyeon balpinda 꼬리가 길면 밟힌다

057》 If your tail is long, somebody is bound to step on it.

Don't leave traces. Don't dwell on something too long.

Kkoriga gilda. Kkori ajik an deuleowatna? 꼬리가 길다. 꼬리 아직 안 들어왔나?

058》 You have a long tail. Or Is your tail not in yet?

Shut the door behind you.

059》 He has broad feet.

Balyi neopda 발이 넓다

A person with good connections. Such an individual is also *madangbal*, or "a foot as large as a front yard." *Madang* is the front yard of a traditional Korean house. Koreans also say a person with large feet has a "thief's feet."

If a housewife has "big hands" (*sonkeuda*), she is generous in her spending and preparation of food for holidays and family parties. Such a woman also has a "large barrel" (*tongkeuda*) or a "wide skirt" (*chimapokyi neopda*).

Share your secrets with a discreet friend, who has a "heavy

mouth" (*ipyi mugeopda*). Never confide in a gossipmonger, who has a "light mouth" (*ipyi gabyeopda*).

If a child has a "short mouth" (*ipyi jjalda*), she is picky about food. If a boy has a "long mouth" (*ipyi gilda*), he eats anything. A boss with a "broad chest" (*gaseumyi neopda*) is big-hearted, while a timid man is a "bird's chest" (*saegaseum*).

A short man is "short dari" – a welding of the English "short" and the Korean "dari," which means leg.

060 » Blood on a bird's foot.

Sae balui pi 새 발의 피

A smidgeon. Or "No problem!"

3 Grit and Hardship

Jammed between bigger powers, Korea developed
an underdog drive to be successful.
Lots of expressions extol pluck and steadfastness.

Maen ttange hedinghagi 맨 땅에 헤딩하기

061 » I'm butting my head on the ground.

Koreans say this when life is tough, or when they take on a challenge with little know-how or few resources but lots of gusto. They mean, "Let's see which will break, my head or the ground."

Mot meokeodo GO! 못 먹어도 고!

062 » I will have a 'go' even if I don't 'eat' it.

I'll go for broke. A term from a Korean card game with an English name: "Go-Stop." When a player tops a certain score, he can quit and collect his profits, saying "Stop!" in English. He "eats" the game. Or he can say "Go!" in English and the game continues with the stakes doubled. The risktaker might preserve his lead, but another player could pass the initial high score and stop the game. In that case, the first player ends up with nothing and has to cough up more cash than the others.

When a player gets to choose whether to stop the game, other cardsharks taunt him. "You should have a go even if you don't eat it, right?" they say.

People often say this when they buy lottery tickets, invest in stocks or take on a project with unclear prospects for success.

"Go-Stop" is the most popular of Korean card games called *hwatu*, or "Battles of Flowers." A deck of cards has 12 suits of four cards each. Each suit is named after a flower such as apricot, cherry and peony.

Gal ttaekkaji gaboja 갈 때까지 가보자

063 》 Let's see how far we can go.

Let's go all the way. This says a lot about South Korea's drinking culture. Drinking sessions often turn into a stamina test. Men barhop for hours before collapsing into a cab on a blurry, neon-lit street. Swaying men clasp each other's shoulders and yell: "Let's have another round. We must go as far as we can."

This pub-lingo is no longer confined to drinkers. People say it when they don't care about the consequences of their acts. In some contexts, "he has gone as far as he can go" means it's time to put a leash on him.

Hwaiting! 화이팅!

064 》 Fighting!

Life as war. South Koreans shout "Fighting!" in English when they cheer sports teams, ship off children to college entrance exams, and toast each other at a team-building office party. Koreans also say "Geonbae" – or "Dry your glass" – when they toast. It means "Bottoms up!"

Expressions of war, or struggle, litter everyday talk. Cars

honk in a "war for parking space" (*juchajeonjaeng*) in Seoul, where traffic is an ordeal.

In an "exam war" (*ipsijeonjaeng*), wealthy parents spend thousands of dollars a month on private tutoring for their children to pass university entrance exams. A diploma from a top university guaranteed a job in big corporations before the economic upheaval of 1997-8. A family's reputation still rises and falls on whether its kids get into college. For days ahead of the exams, mothers pray all night at Buddhist temples and Christian churches. On exam day, always in the winter, mothers bundle up and pray outside the school, some holding prayer beads.

Police go on alert and yank students out of traffic jams so they arrive in time for the exams. The air force cancels training flights to reduce noise during the tests. As exam-takers pile into the school, well-wishers chant "Fighting!"

On big holidays, millions of Koreans hit the roads in a "going home war" (*gwihyangjeonjaeng*). They head for hometowns to perform ancestral rites. What should be a five-hour trip turns into a 20-hour crawl on jammed highways. But Koreans just fill their gas tanks, pack plastic containers with food and, in their words, "go home no matter what."

The origin of all this fighting talk may lie partly in Korea's violent history and the South's underdog drive to succeed in the shadow of two big powers, China and Japan. Koreans endured repression and deprivation during Japan's colonial rule and rose from the ruins of the Korean War to build one of the world's biggest economies.

Gajin geon bulal du jjok 가진 건 불알 두 쪽

065 » All I have is a pair of testicles.

A brash, popular remark that means the speaker doesn't have much to his name, but no shortage of pluck.

Myeonghamdo mot naeminda 명함도 못 내민다

066 » I couldn't even produce my name card.

I was outclassed. In South Korea, you can't do business without a name card. "I have printed my name card" means I have opened a business. "He is going around distributing his name cards" means he is advertising his business.

Nightclub waiters distribute name cards on the streets. In the morning, people find their apartment doors taped with name cards of car sellers, insurance salesmen, milk men, laundry shops and Chinese restaurants.

Korean emphasis on formality and status is reflected in elaborate name cards. Some politicians and businessmen have color photographs printed on name cards, or squeeze in a brief biography: hometown, schools they attended, and various organizations of which they are members.

Koreans love titles. When an elderly man walks into a

coffee shop, the owner often greets him as "Mr. President," even if he's just the proprietor of the grocery store on the corner.

Haneulyi muneojyeodo sotanal gumeongeun itda 하늘이 무너져도 솟아날 구멍은 있다

067 » Even if the sky falls down, there is a hole to escape.

There's always a solution, however bad things look. The phrase testifies to Koreans' capacity for endurance at times of great trial, such as the 1950-53 Korean War. The expression also works when a sports team gets thrashed in a contest. The fans say it while yearning for a miraculous comeback in the remaining rounds.

Hungry jeongsin 헝그리 정신

068 » The spirit of the hungry.

A combination of the English "hungry" and *jeongsin*, the Korean word for "spirit."

The phrase describes the success of a person who overcomes poverty, failure and other hardship. Lim Choon-ae, a female runner, won three gold medals in the 1986 Asian Games. She said she was so poor that she usually ate instant noodles.

She instantly became a national hero. Her success story

deeply touched South Koreans who remembered the hunger and destitution that lingered long after the Korean War.

Older Koreans lament that young people, softened by economic prosperity, no longer remember the "hungry days."

Chiljeonpalgi – or "Knocked down seven times, but rising up eight times" – is a similar term that praises endurance.

South Korean boxing hero Hong Soo-hwan was floored four times before he knocked out Hector Carrasquilla in Panama City in 1977 and won the WBA's junior featherweight championship. His feat created a new phrase: *Sajeonogi*, or "Knocked down four times, but rising up five times."

Ulmyeo gyeoja meokgi 울며 겨자 먹기

069 》 Eating mustard while crying.

Face the music. Koreans don't consume much mustard, though it's spreading fast. It's an essential sauce for *naengmyeon*, or "cold noodles." This Korean favorite is made of buckwheat.

Geodujeolmi 거두절미

070 》 Let's cut the head and tail.

Get straight to the point. A cook chops off the head and tail of a fish because they won't end up in the meal.

A person says this when he wants to talk business right away. Many meetings in Korea begin with name card exchanges, mutual praise and talk of the weather, family, hometown and school connections.

Gujeolyangjang gateun insaeng 구절양장 같은 인생

071 » Life is like the sheep's intestines, folded nine times.

Life is full of ups and downs. About 70 percent of the Korean peninsula is covered by hills. From the top of a mountain, look down and spot a path cut in the slope that twists and bends like intestines. Nine symbolizes a multitude.

Cheopcheopsanjung 첩첩산중

072 » As I walked on, the mountains got taller and more rugged.

The going got tougher. Koreans often compare hardship to climbing mountains, and say a long, difficult journey is like going over "99 hills."

HILL OF BARLEY

The threat of starvation was never distant for peasants who labored under the harsh edicts of their landlords. Spring was especially dreadful. Their winter grain stock was running out and they had to eat roots, tree bark and whatever else was available until the barley harvest in late spring.

Surviving the springtime famine was called "climbing the hill of barley." Once they got over the hill, barley was waiting. Many did not make it.

Hence this tale: An old woman called together her five daughters-in-law to learn who was the wisest. "What is your favorite flower?" she asked. "Rose," one said. "Chrysanthemum," the second said. "Peony," said the third. "Cherry blossom," said the fourth. "The cotton plant," the youngest said.

The old woman then asked the women to name the highest hill on earth. Four gave the names of renowned mountains, but the youngest said, "The hill of barley."

Thus the youngest was declared the wisest. Youths in today's affluent South Korea are unlikely to know the meaning of "hill of barley," but older people use the phrase to describe the hardships of a few decades ago. The suffering persists in North Korea today.

During Japanese colonial rule, peasants surrendered up to 70 percent of their crops in rent and taxes. Most farmers barely made a living as tenants on small plots of land. Many fled and became *hwajeonmin*, "fire-field farmers," who burned off vegetation on remote hills and cultivated small patches of ground before moving elsewhere to repeat the process.

During the spring famine, peasants dug up turnips they had kept in a hole to prevent them freezing during the winter. They made soup with the turnips and whatever grain was left. Some roasted rice husks and pounded them with a little barley to make porridge. Children got stomach ailments from the coarse diet, and their tongues turned black. The colonial government distributed residue left after oil was extracted from beans and sesame seeds, but it did little to ease widespread malnutrition.

Farmers hacked down forests for firewood to warm their houses or barter for grain. Hills remained bare for decades until coal became a principal source of heat, and government-mandated reforestation started in the 1960s. April 5 is South Korea's tree-planting day, a national holiday. Soldiers, government officials and volunteers scale hills to plant trees.

Millions of Koreans emigrated to Manchuria and the Russian Far East to find work and food during colonial rule. The Japanese Imperial Army took 43,000 Koreans to the Far East island of Sakhalin to slave at airfields and coal mines, and most were stranded there for the rest of their lives. After Japanese colonialists withdrew from Korea, the Cold War cut off South Korean migrants from their homeland. Under Josef Stalin, many Koreans in the former Soviet Union were forcibly relocated to central Asia.

Ethnic Koreans abroad began traveling to prosperous South Korea to find work after the country established diplomatic ties with China and Russia in the early 1990s.

Gaettongbate gulreodo iseungyi natda 개똥밭에 굴러도 이승이 낫다

073 》 Even if you roll in a field of dog excrement, this world is better than the next.

Life is worth it, no matter how hard it gets. Korean commoners of old said this, and similar proverbs reflect their rugged attitude:

"Even if you live your life hanging upside down, it's better to live than die."

"It's better to wear rags and crouch in the sun at the street corner than to ride in a big funeral sedan." When a king or rich man died, his family and dozens of porters carried the corpse to the burial site on a large funeral bier decorated with colorful paper and silk.

"You come (to this world) empty-handed and leave empty-handed" (*gongsure, gongsugeo*). However rich you are, you can't take a cent with you when you die.

Samsugapsaneul gadeorado 삼수갑산을 가더라도

074 》 Even if I am sent to Samsu or Gapsan.

No matter what. Ancient kings often banished people to Samsu or Gapsan, two remote, mountainous towns in what is now North Korea. Life was harsh, and many exiles never returned home. Hence "Samsu or Gapsan" became synonymous with a place beyond the bridge of no return. People say, "I must do it even if I am sent to Samsu or Gapsan."

Dak mokeul biteuleodo saebyeokeun onda 닭 목을 비틀어도, 새벽은 온다

075 》 Even if you strangle a cock, the dawn will come anyway.

This remark was made famous by former President Kim Young-sam, once an opposition leader who campaigned against South Korea's military-led governments. Here, the cock symbolizes Korean dissidents' cries for democracy during authoritarian rule.

A shrewd politician, Kim also said: "Politics is a living creature, moving, off on its own." In 1990, he merged his small opposition party with the ruling party of President Roh Tae-woo and won election in late 1992 to become the first civilian president in three decades. His prosecutors jailed Roh and Roh's predecessor and army comrade, Chun Doo-hwan, for corruption and other crimes. He pardoned them just before he left office in early 1998.

Critics said Kim's merger with Roh's ruling party amounted to collusion with a dictator. Supporters said, "You have to enter the tiger's lair to kill it."

Bi on dwie ttangyi dutneunda 비 온 뒤에 땅이 굳는다

076 》 The ground hardens after rain.

After the storm comes the calm.

4 Confucius Said

The Chinese teachings of Confucianism remain a dominant feature of Korean language, behavior and family life.

3
2
1

077》 Man is the seed; woman the field.

This basic rule of Confucian thought explains why all Korean children must inherit the family names of their fathers. Confucianism, the Chinese teachings of devotion to ancestors and family, arrived in Korea in the fourth century and remains the primer in household affairs.

Today, a married woman's name is crossed off her parents' family records and transferred to her husband's. "A married daughter is no longer your child," parents often say. Confucian edicts call for *samjongjido*, or "women obeying three masters:" father, husband and (after the husband's death) eldest son.

Women's groups demand a revision of the civic code, which they deem anachronistic, and have won some legal battles. Sons are no longer entitled to the bulk of their parents' estates, although most fathers still bequeath their assets to their sons, especially the eldest. Few daughters challenge the practice.

In 2001, the men of a family sold a large plot of ancestral real estate and split the money. In an unprecedented case, the family's married daughters demanded their share and sued the men. At the urging of the judge, the family settled and the daughters got some money, though not as much as the amount pocketed by the men.

Stepbrothers who have the same father are called "brothers who came from different bellies." But stepbrothers with the same mother rarely consider themselves brothers. People say the brothers came from "different seeds."

Korean society boasts a strong child-parent bond, but Koreans are reluctant to adopt orphans, whom they call "different blood" or "different seeds."

Cheosamchon bulchohadeut 처삼촌 벌초하듯

078 》 He worked as if he were pruning the grave of his wife's uncle.

He did a slipshod job. Tidying the graves of ancestors is a must in the Confucian code of conduct. Families cut grass on graves during major holidays, but they ignore the final resting places of distant relatives. Relatives on the wife's side are at the bottom of the male-dominated hierarchy.

Sadonui palchon 사돈의 팔촌

079 》 She is my in-law's cousin twice removed.

She and I have virtually no family relationship. Koreans meticulously track down relatives on the father's side of the family. In-laws are considered distant relatives. An elaborate vocabulary expresses the labyrinth of family relations. Calling someone a "cousin," or *sachon*, does not suffice; there are many different terms for cousin, depending on whether the relative is on the father's or mother's side, and is older or younger. There is no word for just "sister" or "brother." There is *hyeong* (older brother) and *dongsaeng* (younger brother), *nuna* (older sister), and *nyeodongsaeng* (younger sister).

Seniority dominates relationships. You had better find out whether your new business partner is older than you so you can use proper vocabulary. If you fail to do that, your counterpart might spread word that you are *beoreut eopneun nom* _ a bastard with bad manners.

Amtatyi ulmyeon jipani manghanda 암탉이 울면 집안이 망한다

080 » If the hen cries, the household will collapse.

A family with a bossy wife is doomed. This implies that only the cock, the husband, is entitled to crow. Wives were once expected to show unconditional devotion to their husbands, a custom that lives on in many a home. Women could not even eat with men at the same table. Instead, they ate separately on the floor or in the kitchen.

Namuraneun sieomeoniboda pyeondeuneun sinuiga deo mipda 나무라는 시어머니보다 편드는 시누이가 더 밉다

081 » You hate the mother-in-law who reproves you. But you hate the sister-in-law who sides with her even more.

You sometimes hate your adversary's ally more than the adversary.

The proverb mirrors the arduous lives of Korean wives of old. The relationship between a woman and her son's wife was one of command and compliance. She and her daughters often joined forces to browbeat the new daughter-in-law, whose aloof husband wasn't much help.

"A mother-in-law who hasn't eaten dinner." A person in a bad mood. Or gloomy weather.

Beongeori samnyeon, gwimeogeori samnyeon 벙어리 삼 년, 귀머거리 삼 년

082 » Dumb for three years, deaf for three years.

A newly wed woman should keep quiet no matter how harshly her husband's family treats her.

When marrying off a daughter, some parents still advise absolute loyalty to the husband's family. According to Confucian edicts, the first of *chilgeojiak* – or "the seven sins for which the husband was entitled to kick out his wife" – was disobedience to the husband's parents. The others were failure to produce children, adultery, jealousy, contracting nasty diseases, talking too much, and thievery. These expressions are still in use, but they don't reflect the greater independence of women today.

Less common expressions: "If you don't do well as a daughter-in-law, even village dogs will look down on you."

"You should break in your new daughter-in-law when she is still in a rainbow dress." A woman used to wear a colorful dress for the first several days of marriage. In a broader context, the phrase means you should dominate a newcomer from the outset.

083 》 A woman who has not died yet.

Mimangyin 미망인

A euphemism for a widow. It once was considered a disgrace for a woman to live longer than her husband, especially when the man died young. The stigma of widowhood is fading in modern Korea, but some conservative parents are still reluctant to let a child marry a widow's offspring, saying "a child who grew up without a father lacks discipline and has bad manners."

Confucian teachings hold that a housewife should not remarry after her husband's death, and numerous widows languished in the days when these codes were strictly enforced. Some widowers and poor bachelors abducted widows at night, wrapping them in white bags and forcibly marrying them later. Such an abduction was called *bossam*, or "wrapping in a bag." A contemporary expression recalls the custom: "She wouldn't notice even if somebody carried her away on his back." She's asleep, out like a light.

Today, *bossam* is a popular dish: steamed pork wrapped in kimchi and consumed with raw oysters.

Haneuleul bwaya byeoleul ttaji 하늘을 봐야 별을 따지

084 》 You must look up and see heaven in order to pluck a star.

First things first. Wives say this about husbands who are seldom home but still complain that they don't have a son. They mean: "If he wants a boy, he should be around so we can sleep together."

In the Confucian view, the husband is heaven. "You must obey your husband just as you look up to heaven" was a common directive for women. Bearing a child, especially a boy, was considered such a sacred duty that it was compared to "plucking a star" from heaven.

Yoejaga haneul pumeumyeon onyuweoledo seoriga naerinda 여자가 한을 품으면 오뉴월에도 서리가 내린다

085 》 A woman who harbors 'han' can make it frost in May and June.

In this context, "han" refers to the determination to seek revenge.

For instance, Koreans believe a mother will stop at nothing to avenge the unjust death of a loved one. Women also use this old phrase as a threat when men try to break up with them.

HAN

A Korean concept, han means resentment, sorrow, sense of loss and hardship, stifled passion and love, or the frustration of the downtrodden, mostly women. It depends on the context.

"I have resolved my han," people declare when they see justice done belatedly, when their sports team beats an archrival, when they pass an exam they have repeatedly flunked, or when they eat something they crave.

In ghost stories, the spirits of the wrongfully slain roam in a Buddhist limbo called *gucheon*, or "Nine Springs," and ask the hero to "resolve their han," or avenge injustice. In movies, a woman dying in her friend's arms asks him to do the same. The anguished hero clenches his fists, looks up to the sky, and declares, "I swear to heaven that I will resolve your han."

Koreans have a cathartic ritual called *hanpulyi*, or "the act of untying han." It can be a solemn, shamanistic dance to console the spirits of the dead, a demonstration against the government or management, or a drinking session during which office workers heap curses on their absent boss.

Han was around well before the 1945 division of the Korean peninsula, but today it captures the agony of elderly Koreans who were separated from their loved ones during the Korean War and have not seen them since. On major holidays, elderly South Koreans travel to the border to gaze at their native North Korea. Some hold ancestral rites with rice and fruits for the parents they left behind.

When students took to the streets in the 1970s and 1980s to demand an end to military rule, they cited the han of *minjung* (masses).

The image that Koreans most associate with han is a woman in white, sighing or wailing over an injustice. Once restricted to working in the fields and kitchen, women had few means of challenging Korea's patriarchal society, and many were denied formal education until the 1950s. An old saying:

"If the mother-in-law scolds her daughter-in-law, the daughter-in-law goes to the kitchen and curses the family dog." The young woman tries to resolve her han on the poor dog.

Yamjeonhan gangaji/goyangyi buttumake meonjeo oreunda 얌전한 강아지 / 고양이 부뚜막에 먼저 올라간다

086 » A tame dog/cat jumps onto the kitchen table.

Sometimes trouble comes from an unlikely source. It most often applies to a meek child who commits an outrageous act or a woman of good name who has an affair. In a similar vein: "There is no murder case that does not involve a woman."

"A tool lent too often breaks; a woman who travels too often gets dirty." A woman's place is in the home.

Weotmulyi malaya araetmulyi malda 윗물이 맑아야 아랫물이 맑다

087 » The water downstream is clean only when the water upstream is clean.

Corruption spreads top down.

Kaljaru 칼자루

088 » He holds the sword hilt.

He has power, especially the authority to fire workers.

Jojikui sseunmat 조직의 쓴 맛

089 » The bitter taste of the organization.

Organized crime rings cited this phrase when punishing a member who betrayed fellow hoods. The underworld slang spread to businesses and government agencies, referring to a maverick employee who was fired or reprimanded.

Chanmul masil ttaedo sunseoga itda 찬물 마실 때도 순서가 있다

090 » There is an order even in drinking cold water.

Seniority rules.

KOREAN HIERARCHY

In old Korea, the family elder got the tastiest morsels and was served first, sitting cross-legged at his tray on the oiled, paper floor. Younger males followed, then women and children. Women served food to the men and ate hastily so they could bring *sungnyung*, or rice tea, to the males at the end of their meal. In winter, the elder sat at the far end of the room where the under-floor flue started and the floor was warmest.

Patriarchal order and seniority prevail today:

● The endings of Korean sentences indicate levels of politeness. Sentences usually end with *yida* (present tense) or *haetda* (past tense). But when the person spoken to is a stranger or is older than the speaker, those sentences end with *ipnida* (present tense) or *hatseupnida* (past tense). *Jinji* and *bap* both mean food in Korean. But you never use *jinji* when you talk to a younger person. *Sul* and *yakju* mean liquor or drink. But *yakju* is only used when speaking to an elderly person in a formal situation. The phrase *bap meokeoteoyo?* – "Have you eaten yet?" – is an equivalent of "Good morning!" But there are several variations of the phrase, depending on the relationship between the speaker and the person addressed. Use the wrong one, and you'll get laughed at or scolded. Most wives address their husbands politely. Men talk down to their spouses.

● During holidays and anniversaries, children kneel before their parents and bow deeply, heads touching the floor.

● Traditionally, parents were stern and strict. Children are expected to be diffident around older people. One spinoff is that many don't make eye contact in conversations. Locking eyes with another person, especially when that person is much older, can be seen as rude or defiant. For example, a girl talking to her school principal tends to look at the floor or her hands.

● Koreans sometimes feign reluctance to take a gift. A hostess who receives a gift from a visitor is apt to say, "Oh why did you bring this?" or even "Why don't you take it back and give it to somebody else?" She doesn't mean it. But reluctance to accept is a form of politeness and humility. In rural areas, this ritual can drag on, with the giver forcing the gift on the hostess. The scene sometimes resembles an argument. When the evening wraps up, the visitor tries to flee the hostess, who chases him and thrusts cash into his pocket, imploring: "Please take this and pay for the cab."

● Koreans don't gesture much when speaking with the elderly. They usually stand erect, or sit with their hands in front of them. They talk little, waiting until the older person invites them to speak.

● It is considered rude to smoke in the presence of elderly people. Never smoke with your father or uncles, no matter how old you are. A polite man offers his lighter with two hands to light an older man's cigarette. When drinking, the younger man holds the bottle with both hands and fills the older man's glass. He rarely fills his own glass, instead waiting until the older man offers to fill it. He holds his glass with both hands to receive the offering. He usually drinks with his head turned away from an elderly man to show respect.

● In most offices, people address each other by title. They say, "Mr. Manager Kim" or "Mr. Manager," but rarely just "Mr. Kim." Dark suits and ties, or maybe a jacket with the company logo, are a virtual office uniform. Everybody gets promoted at the same time, and salary increases are all the same. At the end

of the day, everyone sits at their desks, fidgeting and waiting for their superiors to leave so they can too.

● Officials sometimes use terms reminiscent of the old royal court. In 2001, a personal memo of the newly appointed justice minister came to light. In the memo, he called his appointment "glory to my family" and thanked President Kim Dae-jung's "royal favor as great as a big mountain," a stock phrase used by ancient court officials. The embarrassed minister quit after a few days in office.

● Observers of North Korea remark that the isolated country is as Confucian as it is communist. North Koreans refer to their ruler, Kim Jong Il, as "Dear Father" or "Great Leader." The North's state-run propaganda machine depicts him as a "faithful son" of his father, late President Kim Il Sung.

Chanmul meokgo yi ssusinda 찬물 먹고 이 쑤신다

091 » Picking teeth after drinking water. Or He belched like a dragon after eating a loach.

All for show. Commoners of old cited these phrases to ridicule the image-conscious yangban, the noble class of Korea's Yi Dynasty. In "Yangban Jon," a satirical novella of that era, a rich man tries to buy a yangban title for 1,000 bushels of rice. The man gives up and flees after hearing how a noble had to behave.

"A yangban must get up by 5 a.m., look down the tip of his nose when talking to others, swallow phlegm, speak in a drawl, and walk slowly, dragging the heels of his shoes on the ground," the local magistrate tells the rich man. "A yangban should not touch money with bare hands, should not take off his padded socks even if it's hot, should not take off his hat even when he is eating, should not ask the price of rice, should not make noise when eating or putting down his chopsticks, should not lick at his beard after drinking rice wine, should not suck in his cheeks when smoking...."

Suyeomyi seokjarado meokeoya yangban 수염이 석자라도 먹어야 양반

092 » Even if you have a three-foot-long beard, you must eat to remain yangban.

Don't be picky about food. The phrase also applies to a man who neglects basic obligations, such as providing for his family, and concentrates instead on unrealistic goals.

Yangban, the old elite, roughly means "those divided into two groups." When a king presided over his court, he faced south. Heads bowed, court ministers stood in two rows – one on the king's left and the other on his right.

A yangban man and a servant got lost deep in the woods and their food ran out. Both were famished, but the master refused to eat rotten potatoes brought by his servant, chastising him for offering food below his status. The servant persisted: "Sir, please eat this. Although you have a three-foot-long beard, you must eat to live. If you die, you are nothing; you won't be yangban anymore."

YANGBAN

Yangban owned the land while commoners labored to pay rent with their rice crop. The gentlemen grew long beards as a symbol of prestige, wore horsehair hats and smoked slender bamboo pipes lit by servants. They led a leisurely existence of hunting and other pastimes. They paced slowly, hands clasped behind their backs. They wrote poems, enjoyed literature and studied Confucianism and other Chinese philosophy. When a yangban child went to school, a servant trailed behind with textbooks.

Yangban men were sometimes more thorough than their Chinese teachers in their strict adherence to Confucian family values. Discouraged from leaving their homes, yangban wives handled household chores, sewed and embroidered. Unmarried women who ventured outside often wore a hood.

Commoners viewed the yangban with both scorn and admiration. The following proverbs could either ridicule absurd formalities or stress the merits of dignified behavior at times of duress.

"Even if freezing to death, the yangban would never come close to a rice straw fire." The fire worthy of the yangban is made with smokeless charcoal.

"Even if he were drowning, the yangban would not swim like a dog." A Korean gentleman would supposedly risk his life to defend his dignity, or *chaetong*.

The Russians and Japanese conscripted sons of elite families into their armies when they competed for control of Korea in the late 19th century. Some yangban boys appeared at their first military exercises on the backs of servants. When the boys marched, the servants followed with chamber pots.

Mot oreul namu chyeodabojido mara 못 오를 나무 쳐다보지도 마라

093 » If you can't climb a tree, you shouldn't look up at it.

Don't dream of something beyond your means. Generations ago, this saying was a warning to commoners not to challenge the noble class.

Today, an aloof woman might tell her suitors that they are "looking at a tree they cannot climb."

Motsaengin beolre moro ginda 못생긴 벌레 모로 긴다

094 》 An ugly worm crawls sideways.

If you can't stand someone, you even hate the way he walks. The "ugly worm" is a scoundrel who draws uneasy stares, or a maverick who doesn't slot into a conformist organization.

Jireongyido baleumyeon kkumteul 지렁이도 밟으면 꿈틀

095 》 Even an earthworm wiggles when someone steps on it.

The weak lash out when the strong do them injustice.

KOREAN MASSES

In old Korea, people lived in clusters of mud-and-thatch huts at the foot of rugged hills, tending rice paddies in the valleys. They worked hard in summer, ahead of the autumn harvest, and retreated in winter into the silence of their snow-covered huts. They feared bandits, tax collectors, rumors of foreign invaders and beasts prowling down the mountains at night. Grain stores dwindled by the spring, when peasants began collecting sprouts and edible roots.

Over the centuries, Koreans endured numerous invasions. The Chinese subdued them on the few occasions when they stirred from their subjugation and rode into Manchuria to seize territory. Manchurian tribes sought Korea for plunder or space to escape from expanding Chinese empires. Horsemen from the Mongolian steppes terrorized the Asian continent all the way to its eastern tip and corraled the Korean kings into an island off the peninsula's west coast. Japan saw Korea as a stepping stone for advance into China or just a place to plunder and defuse tension among its bickering warlords.

Koreans sometimes routed foreign expeditions several times the size of their native army, but their brief victories were usually followed by an even bigger invasion that swept the peninsula. The Chinese kept a vigilant eye on the Koreans, whom they called "people in white" because of their white garb, or "people who like singing and dancing." In Korea, village festivals were boisterous. The rigors of agriculture demanded that villagers depend on each other, and this solidarity translated into collective resistance in times of crisis. Small groups of farmer-guerrillas often harassed foreign invaders.

The exuberance of commoners contrasted with the constrained emotion and decorum of the ruling class. The yangban listened to musicians who twanged sleepy tunes on zithers for hours. The masses danced to the jaunty rhythm of drums and gongs, and celebrated harvests with vulgar clowning and jokes about their landlords. The heart-thumping throb, clang, and boom of their instruments are a fixture at many a protest and festival today.

Japanese-invented karaoke is more popular in modern South Korea than anywhere else in the world. A reveler who skips a turn at the microphone is a party pooper.

"If you don't come out, we will invade you," the rest of the group chants, comparing their reluctant friend to a timid enemy holed up in a castle.

Villagers once staged mock battles, wielding long poles and hurling stones at each other. Stones and sticks were the main protest tools when students and workers clashed with the security forces of authoritarian governments from the 1960s until democratic reforms in the late 1980s. Fists clenched, the protesters said:

Chamneun daedo hangaega itda, or "There's a limit to a man's patience."

Most slogans at South Korean demonstrations comprise four syllables. Protesters spit out the syllables, accentuating each one with a raised fist. *Dok-jae-ta-do!* (Down with dictatorship!), *Yang-key-go-home!* (Yankee go home!), or *Go-yong-bo-jang!* (We want jobs!)

Gumbaengyido gureuneun jaejuga itda 굼뱅이도 구르는 재주가 있다

096 » A grub has the skill of rolling.

Everybody has his worth. The expression is a tribute to down-and-outs who survive all manner of hardship. It also applies to someone, once thought hopeless, who succeeds.

Gakha, siweonhasigetsumnida 각하, 시원하시겠습니다

097 » Your highness, you must feel relieved now!

An earnest Cabinet minister is rumored to have said this when President Syngman Rhee farted loudly during a Cabinet meeting. The story was never confirmed, but the phrase became a favorite among South Koreans eager to ridicule authoritarian leaders and their underlings.

Rhee became South Korea's founding president in 1948 amid widespread instability fomented by leftist activists. That year, communist guerrillas attacked police stations in an uprising in the southernmost island of Jeju. Rhee's forces killed thousands of islanders in a "scorched earth" operation to root out rebels and their supporters.

Rhee's end came in 1960 when students rose up in major cities, chanting "Down with Dictatorship!" to protest alleged vote-rigging that helped Rhee win his fourth term as president. Public fury grew when the body of a student was found floating in a harbor, a police tear gas canister stuck in his eye socket. Rhee's police killed nearly 200 people, mostly students, across the nation. But the protests escalated, and Rhee fled into exile in Hawaii.

Nimdo bogo ppongdo ttago 님도 보고 뽕도 따고

098 》 She both picked mulberries and saw her lover.

She killed two birds with one stone. A woman told her parents that she was going out to pick mulberries. She and her boyfriend had earlier agreed to meet in the mulberry field.

Showing romantic affection in public was a taboo in old Korea. A girl who came across a boy in a village alley stepped aside and averted her eyes. If their glances met, the girl blushed. Tales abound about girls and boys meeting in secret. Marriage was almost always arranged by parents, who hired matchmakers and fortunetellers to check family backgrounds and study whether *saju gunghap*, or horoscopes, of the young couple matched. In many cases, the bride and groom never saw each other until wedding day.

Chimatbaram 치맛바람

099 》 Skirt wind.

Women's brisk social activities. Women of old wore long, flowing dresses called *hanbok*. If they moved briskly, the long skirts caught the wind like a sail.

The term gained notoriety during rapid economic growth in

the 1970s and 1980s, when wealthy housewives traveled together, dropping fortunes on real estate speculation. Conservative men cite this term to express disapproval of socially active women.

Today, few women work in the top levels of government or pursue a sustained career. Most devote themselves to household work after marriage, and find it hard to get an office job. Many sell insurance policies, a profession shunned by most men who prefer desk jobs. In many families, the duties of child care and household affairs fall entirely on wives, while husbands focus on their jobs. Men are not supposed to enter the kitchen. Husbands rarely cook or help their wives wash dishes. Fathers rarely show up for group meetings with teachers at their children's school. Some conservative men consider it below their dignity to carry a shopping basket.

Ajuma 아줌마

100 》 Ajuma.

A married woman, often a restaurant worker, street vendor or middle-aged housewife. You seldom call the wife of your boss "ajuma" because of its stereotypical image: a loud, bustling woman in mismatched clothing. Never call an unmarried woman "ajuma," and young, married women don't like the term either. Yet most Koreans admire the ajuma's hard work and aggressiveness. Market ajumas wear baggy pants, little makeup and towels wrapped around their heads. They often carry goods on their heads. They are raucous and cuss rude men. Most ajuma come from poor backgrounds, but they are eager to educate their children, considering college diplomas a way to elevate their families' social status. Some push and shove their way through a crowd to find a seat in the bus or subway. Such behavior led some social commentators to dub ajuma "a third sex," neither woman nor man.

"Ajumeoni" is a politer term than ajuma, and can refer to virtually any middle-aged or older woman.

5 CHARACTERS

Korean is crowded with figures
who leap to life from history,
old novels and folk tales.

101 » Water demon.

Mulgwisin 물귀신

A doomed person who is determined to drag you down as well. "You die! I die!" the water demon might say. But the label can be a term of grudging admiration for a persistent character.

An underdog who keeps bouncing back to damage a more powerful opponent employs "the strategy of a water demon."

In Korean lore, the water demon pulls a swimmer into the depths, then allows the flailing victim to swim toward shore. Feet almost touching the bottom, the quarry is pulled down again. The monster plays the game until the exhausted victim perishes.

Daedonggangmuldo pala meokeul saram 대동강물도 팔아 먹을 사람

102 » He could sell the water of the Daedong River.

He could flog the Brooklyn Bridge. This expression comes from the legend of Kim Sun Dal, who learned that a wealthy but obtuse businessman from Seoul was visiting Pyongyang, now the capital of North Korea. Kim went to the Daedong River, which flows through the city, and bought drinks for men who were drawing water. He distributed coins and asked the men to pretend to pay him for the water. Rumor spread and the Seoul businessman, spotting a bottomless source of income, offered to buy the river. Kim sold it for 4,000 coins.

103 » Ink-pad box. Meoktong 먹통

A blockhead. To design furniture, old-style carpenters use a small box filled with ink-soaked cotton. A thread goes into the box and comes out stained black. The builder pulls out the thread and marks straight lines on a wooden plank. The ink-pad box, which stains anything that goes through it, became a synonym for a person who ignores common sense. Today it more often refers to a telephone on the blink or a crashed PC. "My computer turned into an ink-pad box again!" shouts a flustered office worker.

104 » You look like a sack of borrowed barley. Kkwedanon borigatyi 꿔다 논 보리같이

A wallflower. An ill-at-ease guest at a gathering. A borrowed sack of barley sits in a peasant's house, inviting uneasy glances from family members for whom the sack is a constant reminder of their poverty.

105 » A dish that has too little salt. Eolganyi 얼간이

A dimwit.

106 » Eolreri, kkolreri.

Eolreri, kkolreri 얼레리, 꼴레리

Kids tease a friend, chanting "Eolreri, kkolreri." They often do this with their index fingers pointing at their cheeks, tongues protruding.

Eolreri derives from *Alari*, which in old Korean meant "a baby government official," a derogatory term for an inexperienced magistrate. *Kkolreri* has no meaning, but adds rhythm.

107 » A woman who returned home.

Hwanyangnyeon 화냥년

A promiscuous woman, or one who is having an extramarital affair. It's also an expletive equivalent to "bitch" in English.

The phrase stems from the invasion of Korea by China's Ching Dynasty in the winter of 1636-7. The Korean Yi Dynasty's King In Jo abandoned Seoul and retreated to a castle south of the capital as Chinese troops plundered the country. The besieged monarch finally surrendered, kneeling and pledging allegiance to the Chinese king at a Han River ferry station in one of the most humiliating moments in Korean history.

The Chinese abducted many Koreans, incarcerating them and demanding ransoms from their families. Many were sold as slaves and worked to buy their freedom. Korean women who returned from the ordeal were treated as outcasts because many had been raped by Chinese soldiers. They were called *hwan hyangnyeo*, or "women who returned home." Over the centuries, the term changed to *hwanyangnyeon*, taking on the derogatory suffix for a woman: *nyeon*.

Some returning women brought babies that were both pitied and resented. They were called *horojasik*, or "children of barbarians." Now the phrase simply means "bastards." *Hwa nyangnyeon* and *horojasik* are two of the worst insults in South Korea.

Korean kings paid tributes to China until the late 19th century.

Decades before the Chinese invasion, Japanese troops abducted Koreans and took with them the ears and noses – preserved in salt – of tens of thousands of slaughtered Koreans. The war booty was later buried. The "Tomb of Ears" still stands in Kyoto, an ancient Japanese capital. Korean tour guidebooks urge Koreans to visit.

108 》 Fluorescent light.

Hyeonggwangdeung 형광등

A person slow to understand, like a neon light that flickers a few times before lighting up.

109» Soviet submachine gun.

Ttabalchong 따발총

A nonstop talker. During the Korean War, North Korean troops carried 7.62 mm Soviet submachine guns with a disk-shaped magazine. Koreans called the burp gun *ttabalchong*, or "a gun with a coiled pad." The gun's magazine reminded Koreans of *ttabal*, the ring-shaped head pad that women used to carry loads on their heads.

The gun could fire 900 rounds per minute. Now *ttabal chong* means a person who spews words like bullets.

110» I-don't-know guy.

Mo Ro Soe 모로쇠

An enigma. If a man accused of bribery says he doesn't remember anything, Koreans call him "Mo Ro Soe." The "I-don't-know guy" is a much-loathed character. The old "Story of Mo Ro Soe" is an exercise in contradiction. It begins:

"There lived a man called Mo Ro Soe. He was blind but could find a dog's hair fallen to the ground. He was deaf but could hear ants wrestling. He was dumb, but when he opened his mouth, words poured out in a cascade."

It goes on: "One day, while working in a snow-covered summer field, he was bitten by a three-legged snake, which ate his scythe. His face swelled like a mountain. Running to the village to ask what to do, he met a Buddhist nun. When he asked her for help, she stroked her long white beard and said, 'Go and find soot in a fireplace that has never been used, and get a pubic hair of an old prostitute that has never been sullied.'"

The ludicrous tale goes on and on, until the narrator ends: "I don't know what the hell I am talking about."

111 » Bellows. Heopungseonyi 허풍선이

A gasbag, braggart. Bellows are *heopungseonyi*, or "a fan that makes fake winds."

"He is fanning fake winds" (*heopungchinda*) means he is blowing his own trumpet.

112 » Military adviser. Gomungwan 고문관

An oaf. At the end of World War II, American troops and military advisers disembarked in South Korea to disarm Japanese colonial soldiers. The advisers helped assemble and train a South Korean military. Koreans found their manners odd, and laughed at the accents of the few Americans who tried to speak a smattering of Korean. Some visitors walked into Korean houses with their shoes on, a gaffe in many Asian societies. They fumbled with their chopsticks and grimaced in discomfort if they sat cross-legged on the floor. Some fell victim to local grifters.

Soon, South Korean soldiers were describing gawky comrades as “military advisers.” Since all South Korean men must serve in the military, the term found a niche in civilian jargon. Now it means anybody whose incompetence undermines teamwork.

Those early American advisers brought with them ‘Field Manuals,’ or FMs, which survive in Korean jargon.

FMdaero haja! “Let’s do it according to FMs!” means “Let’s do it by the book!”

113》 One who picks sleeves.

Somaechigi 소매치기

A pickpocket. In old Korea, a pickpocket picked sleeves. The traditional *hanbok* costume had big baggy sleeves resembling a pelican’s pouch. People kept cash and letters in their voluminous sleeves, which served as pockets. In the late 19th century, the government ordered the elite class, yangban, to trim their sleeves, which had become a symbol of bribe-taking.

114》 Mr. Byeon Gang Soe.

Byeon Gang Soe 변강쇠

A gigolo. A man of great sexual prowess. A raunchy folk tale dwells on the astounding sexual stamina of Byeon Gang Soe. The fictitious character and an equally promiscuous woman, Ong Nyeo, settle together in a remote mountain valley. Too lazy to cut down trees, Byeon pulls out village totem poles called "jangseung" to use for firewood. Outraged totem poles across the country call an urgent meeting to consider a punishment for Byeon. They afflict him with pus, fever, gangrene and other diseases. Byeon dies a gruesome death, standing up, unable to close his eyes, his mouth stretched in a frozen howl.

Today Byeon Gang Soe refers to sexual prowess, not the character's hideous fate.

JANGSEUNG

Jangseung are Korean totem poles carved with scary figures with names such as "Great General Under the Heaven" or "Great Woman General Under the Ground." The generals once stood in pairs at village entrances, repelling evil spirits and providing safe passage for travelers, who bowed before the posts. Mothers and wives whose men were traveling laid rice cakes, rice wine or dried fish at the feet of the poles. Jangseung were road guardians and served as road signs on the boundaries of towns and counties.

"Why are you standing like jangseung?" is a question for a tall man who stands silently.

Jangseung poles are usually pine and chestnut tree trunks, about 10 feet tall. The top of a typical one is carved into a face with bulging eyes, a big, bulbous nose, snaggleteeth, a long beard and a gaping hole of a mouth. The sinewy shape of the crooked pine tree adds to the totem pole's intimidating look. The stooping figures stare down reproachfully. Many a village kid shuddered on approaching these figures at dusk. Grandmothers warned the young:

"The jangseung will hoist itself out of the ground and fly after you if you don't behave."

No two totem poles look the same. Their shapes and names reflect Buddhist, Confucian, Taoist or animist beliefs and the artistic touch of their makers. Their faces grin, sneer or frown, depending on what angle you look at them. Buddhist monks and Confucian scholars tolerated the homegrown spiritual symbols, but many disappeared after the arrival of Christianity in Korea in the 19th century. Some rural villages still have jangseung.

The southern island of Jeju preserved stone totems called *dolharubang*, or "stone grandfathers." They are lumpy statues of an old man with bulging eyes, long ears, closed mouth and a rimless hat. He keeps his shoulders high and his clenched hands at the sides of his belly, as if he were about to throw a punch at the onlooker. The statue is the mascot of the resort island.

115 » Village drum. Dongnebuk 동네북

An easy target, pushover. A village drum belongs to the community and anyone can beat it. When bullies rough up a kid in the schoolyard, the victim wonders: "Am I a village drum?"

A sports context: "Our team has become the village drum; everybody beats us."

116 » Beans and barley. Ssukmaek 쑥맥

A dunce, especially one who is awkward around women. There was a man who couldn't tell beans from barley, no matter how hard he tried.

117 » King's envoy to Hamheung. Hamheungchasa 함흥차사

A person who goes on an errand but is never heard from again. "My son went to fetch some sugar from the shop an hour ago," a mother says. "I wonder what happened. He must have become an envoy to Hamheung."

Yi Sung-ke, a Koryo Dynasty general, founded the Yi Dynasty in 1392 and became its first king. He never got along with his son, Bang-won, who engineered a palace coup and took power in 1400. Yi Sung-ke retired to Hamheung, a remote seaside town in what is now North Korea. Bang-won sent envoys to reconcile with his father, but the old man either killed or detained them.

Bang-won was determined to win over his father to ensure his own royal legitimacy, and his chance came when an elderly court minister of the former king volunteered to visit him. The minister went alone on an old horse, along with its pony. Near Yi Sung-ke's home, he tied the pony to a tree and continued on the horse, which kept looking back at its whinnying offspring. Yi saw this and asked what was going on. The envoy said a parent and child should never separate. Impressed, Yi told his ex-minister that he would return home.

The minister himself never made it home; he was murdered by Yi's aides against the wishes of the former king.

118 » Executioner. Mangnani 망나니

A rascal, especially one who mistreats his parents. The executioner of old Korea was *mangnani*, or "a person of disgraced origin."

The man who cut off heads for a living belonged to the lowest social caste. His hair was disheveled and his chest bared during an execution. He performed the "executioner's dance," stomping wildly around the condemned, brandishing a huge, curved sword and spouting water onto the glinting blade.

119 ›› One who eats rice but does nothing else.

Babo 바보

The most common term for fool. A derivative slang term *baptong* – or a container for cooked rice – means a glutton, or good-for-nothing. "You're just reducing our rice supply" is a common barb. Such a person is also *sikchungyi*, or "a bug that eats rice."

120 ›› Acorns in dog food.

Gaebape dotori 개밥에 도토리

Outcasts. Throw a few acorns along with dog food into a bowl, and the dog will slurp up the contents, jowls flapping. But it won't touch those acorns.

Yakbange gamcho 약방에 감초

121 ›› Licorice in the herb doctor's shop.

An indispensable item or person. Or a know-it-all who pokes into everybody's business.

Licorice is an ingredient in virtually every prescription by traditional Korean herb doctors. Its sweet taste tones down the herbalist's bitter, black liquid concoctions. Herb doctors deal in centuries-old prescriptions. They perform acupuncture and burn cones of crushed, dried stalks of mugwort on a patient's skin to relieve backaches and other troubles.

Most homegrown remedies are no longer practiced. Many years ago, a child with hiccups was forced to swallow a live loach without washing it down with water.

Eokkaedongmu 어깨동무

122 》 Shoulder friend.

A childhood friend. Buddies used to hook their arms around each other's shoulders. Another term is "a testicle friend." The inference is that close friends once played together naked in the water in summertime, their genitals fully exposed.

Anjeunjarie puldo an nanda 앉은자리에 풀도 안 난다

123 》 Even weeds wouldn't grow where she sat.

She doesn't compromise. Or, "Even a tiger would spit him out."

Mule mul tandeut, sule sul tandeut 물에 물 탄 듯, 술에 술 탄 듯

124 》 Like water mixed with water, like wine mixed with wine.

Mixing water with water, and wine with wine, won't make a

difference. A reference to a weak, indecisive person.

Gen. Roh Tae-woo helped his comrade, Gen. Chun Doo-hwan, take power in a 1979 coup and succeeded him as president in 1988. Critics ridiculed Roh as "Mul Tae-woo," or Mr. Water. Roh called himself an "ordinary man," and promised a "government for ordinary people." He told skeptics, "Please believe in this man." The soft-voiced Roh seemed meek and vacillating compared to his gritty predecessors, Chun and Park Chung-hee. Some Koreans grumbled that he didn't have any backbone or charisma. Roh's supporters note that during his tenure, South Korea opened diplomatic ties with Russia and China and adopted democratic reforms ahead of the transfer of power to a civilian president in 1993.

Chun and Roh were arrested in 1995 for corruption, the 1979 coup and a bloody military crackdown on a pro-democracy uprising in 1980. A few years later, they were pardoned. Chun and Roh remained popular in their home provinces, where people believed their imprisonment was politically motivated.

Mokseok 목석

125 » The man who is made of wood and stone.

A callous man. A determined man of principle. Or a man who appears indifferent to sexual temptation.

126 》 A dumb person who ate honey.

Someone who's desperate to communicate, but can't. Once a dumb man got sick after eating too much honey. His wife found the man rolling in agony, and asked what had happened. The dumb man pointed his finger at the honey jar, and the wife brought more honey to his lips.

Disabled people carry a stigma under Confucian tenets that revere the purity of a whole body inherited from ancestors. Old Korean noblemen grew their beards and kept their hair in topknots, rarely cutting them. They wrapped cut hair and fingernails in clean cloth before disposal.

Koreans are reluctant to donate blood or organs. Red Cross buses visit railway stations, military units and schools to urge young people to donate blood, which is in short supply in hospitals. Civic leaders launched a campaign to donate their organs when they die, and urged people to follow suit. On the walls of hospital bathrooms, the family of a patient who urgently needs a kidney transplant might find cellular telephone numbers of people willing to sell one of their kidneys – or brokers of such deals. Those transactions are illegal.

"I felt like a blind man who lost his walking stick." A hopeless situation.

"I felt like a dumb person with a heartache." You've got a problem but can't complain.

"He found it the way a blind man finds a doorknob." He got lucky.

127 》 Mr. Ong Ko Jip. Ong Ko Jip 옹고집

A stubborn, miserly character. In "The Story of Ong Ko Jip," the protagonist mistreats his sick mother. Whenever a Buddhist monk comes to his house to beg for food, he beats and humiliates the holy man by piercing his ear lobes.

A vengeful monk makes the man's effigy with rice straw and gives it life. The replica enters the house and forces out the real Ong Ko Jip. The straw man lives happily with Ong Ko Jip's wife, who gives birth to several children. Another monk later draws a talisman for the ousted man. When Ong Ko Jip returns to his house and shows the talisman, the straw man and his children explode. After the smoke clears, the rest of the family sees only a stack of straw. The real man reclaims his wife and house and becomes a good son to his old mother and a kind host to itinerant monks.

"He is an Ong Ko Jip" means he is as stubborn as a mule.

Donge beonjjeok seoeh beonjjeok 동에 번쩍 서에 번쩍

128 》 Hardly had he flashed by in the east when he flashed by in the west.

A busybody who makes a lot of appearances all over the place. The phrase is attributed to the protagonist of a 17th-century novel who can shrink space and transform himself into whatever he wants to be. The "Story of Hong Kil Dong" was the first novel written in the Korean alphabet. This classic treated a major social issue during the Yi Dynasty: discrimination against the children of noblemen's concubines. The offspring were barred from working in the government or inheriting their fathers' wealth.

In the novel, Hong is the illegitimate son of an elite family. He flees his home, learns magic and becomes Korea's Robin Hood, stealing from the rich and distributing booty to the poor. When soldiers come to arrest him, he confuses them with numerous replicas of himself. Because of his ability to contract space, he "appears and disappears like a ghost" in several places at the same time. Hong reconciles with the royal court and serves as defense minister. He eventually sails across a sea and builds his own kingdom free of class discrimination.

129 » The brother of kisaeng.

Kisaeng orabi 기생오라비

Originally, a pimp. Now a libertine who hangs around bars and night clubs, or just any slippery character. The stereotype has oiled, slicked back hair.

Kisaeng, which is pronounced *kee-sehng,* is a female entertainer who sang, danced and served drinks at parties in old Korea.

KISAENG

Generations ago, the sexes rarely mixed past the age of seven, except for close family. Women were discouraged from talking to men, and aloof husbands conversed with wives only when necessary.

Upper-class men addressed their wives with formal language, and rarely ate meals with their spouses. Those men, however, enjoyed female entertainers called "kisaeng," the equivalent of the Japanese geisha.

Poor parents sold pretty daughters to training schools for entertainers, hoping they could avoid a life of toil in the fields. The girls were trained to be submissive servants as well as gracious hostesses. They learned how to dance, sing, play musical instruments and read and write poems. The training made kisaeng one of the most cultivated groups of women in old Korea, yet they belonged to one of the lowest classes of the social caste. They contravened Confucian edicts that a woman serves only one man. Confucianism also showed little regard for music and dancing, which were called "miscellaneous arts."

Kisaeng wore makeup and colorful silk dresses and piled their hair in coiffures. On the street, they wore distinctive caps resembling small, elaborate umbrellas. They were not afraid to show their faces and talk to men.

The government hired and trained some kisaeng, while others studied medicine and worked as nurses and doctors in the royal palaces. Many were prostitutes.

Several kisaeng became famous poets. In 1919, a group of kisaeng demanded independence in a demonstration against Japanese colonialists.

Local Korean officials stopped hiring and training kisaeng toward the end of Japanese colonial rule in 1910-45.

Defectors from North Korea alleged that leader Kim Jong Il had his own "entertainment squad" (*gippeumjo*), a group of pretty, highly skilled female entertainers who perform at his parties.

6
Tough Talk

Terms about death and murder abound in Korea,
the stage for many a foreign invasion and civil war.
When Koreans sound combative,
they don't always mean what they say.

130 » You die! I die! Ni jukgo nae jukja 니죽고 내죽자

Imagine Koreans hissing this threat with clenched fists and bared teeth. They're determined to get their way at whatever cost. At least, that's the impression they want to give. Maybe they're bluffing. In drunken brawls, men growl "You die! I die!" Housewives scream it when their drunken spouses stagger home late at night. Mothers scold their children with it when the kids don't behave or study.

One famous Korean in the 16th century who practiced this strategy was Non Ke, a "kisaeng," or female dancer and entertainer. Chinju, a south-coast town where she was working, was one of the last Korean bastions to fall to a Japanese invasion force. The Japanese general threw a victory feast on a pavilion overlooking Chinju's Nam River. Korean kisaeng were ordered to sing and dance. Non Ke was determined to avenge many Koreans who committed suicide before the surrender of their castle to avoid rape or execution by the Japanese. During the party, she plied the enemy general with alcohol and lured him to a cliff. She embraced the intoxicated commander. Her rings interlocked when she clasped her hands behind his back. She stepped off the cliff, and they both plunged to their deaths in the river far below. Non Ke is a national hero.

The "You die! I die!" philosophy may suggest how heavily armed South and North Korea have maintained an uneasy standoff for so many years. The two halves know that another conflict like the Korean War could be even more devastating. A large U.S. troop deployment in the South guards against the North, which has a formidable arsenal, much of it near the inter-Korean border.

It's never "I die! You die!" "You die!" comes first.

Han beon jukji du beon jukna 한 번 죽지 두 번 죽나

131 » You only die once, not twice.

Daredevils say this before a challenge. They also say: *Jukyi ani myeon, kkamura chigi*, or "I will either die or faint."

132 » You can slash open my belly.

Bajjaera! 배째라!

A friend says this after wolfing down the snack you set aside to munch on later. He means: "What's done is done. What are you going to do about it?" A swindler facing a jail term says this if he doesn't plan to cough up the money.

Some villains even try to shift the blame. The phenomenon is *jeokbanhajang*, or "A thief picks up the bat against the owner of the house and yells 'Thief!'"

Nae nune heuk deureogagi jeone 내 눈에 흙 들어가기 전에

133 » Not until dirt enters my eyes!

Over my dead body.

Jukinda/Juknunda/Jukko sipnya? 죽인다 / 죽는다 / 죽고 싶냐?

134 » I will kill you Or You will die Or Do you want to die?

Koreans don't really mean it. They just want to get their point across, often with a smile: "Hey, don't be late. You'll die if you are." Or a mother says to her son: "Why don't you study? Do you want to die?"

The homicide rate in Korea is relatively low. Private gun ownership is banned in most cases, though every man serves 26 months in the military as a conscript. But South Korea is awash in expressions involving murder, death and execution. If ignored, Koreans say they "were killed by silence." (*muksal*). A beautiful woman is "brain-killing" (*noesal*). *Malsal*, or "killing by erasing," means dismissing something or someone.

More aggressive expressions are known as *akdam*, or "evil discourse." "Get out and die!" (*naga jukeora!*) "He deserves death by beating!" (*ttaeryeo jukiyl nom!*) "He will be hit by lightning!" (*byeorak maja jukeul nom!*) Or "He will get scabies on his liver and die without even scratching them."

Balgarake kkin ttaeboda mothan geot 발가락에 낀 때보다 못한 것

135 » You're worse than the dirt between my toes.

You are nobody.

Ttonggae hurlyeosikinya? 똥개 훈련시키냐?

136 » Are you training a mongrel dog?

A sarcastic expression of revolt. A devil-may-care office minion says this to a pushy boss.

Gaeboda mothan nom 개보다 못한 놈

137 » He is no better than a dog.

A universal insult, but Koreans have a repertoire of stories about good dogs. One tells of a mutt that saved its drunken master, who fell asleep in the woods. The forest caught fire. The dog ran to a pond, doused its fur, scampered back to fight the flames and licked its master, who didn't stir from his stupor. When the man finally woke up, he found his faithful dog at his side, dead from burns and exhaustion.

Koreans used to build monuments to "faithful dogs." Some dog statues still stand in rural towns.

The dog is a favorite pet in Korea. Some women carry coiffed dogs in bags or jackets.

Certain kinds of dogs are bred for their meat, which is said to enhance the sexual prowess of men. They are called "brown dogs" in Korean. Canine flesh is usually served in a "tonic soup" (*bosintang*).

International animal rights groups condemn the custom, but Koreans bristle at such criticism. Although most Koreans don't eat dog, office workers in crisp shirts and ties bunch into restaurants in Seoul to slurp dog meat soup on summer days. Concerned about its international image, South Korea banned dog restaurants during the 1988 Seoul Olympics, temporarily invoking a law that banned sales of "unsightly food."

Dog meat is especially popular in North Korea, where it is called *dangogi*, or "sweet meat."

Boknal gae paedeuthada 복날 개 패듯하다

138 》 They beat him like a dog on a 'bok' day.

They gave him a good thrashing. *Bok* refers to a hot summer day. The Korean lunar calendar has three *bok* days _ the hottest days of the year. On these days, Koreans eat dog to fight fatigue. People also say, "I will beat you up like a dog in May and June." The dog-eating season begins in May.

A villager hanged a dog by the neck from a tree and bludgeoned it to death with a bat. The method was said to soften the flesh. The practice is disappearing today. Most butchers slaughter dogs with electric shocks, ensuring almost instant death.

"Sell your dogs!" shouted dog traders in the countryside

around *bok* season. They used to roam villages on motorbikes with metal cages on the back seats, and still do in some out-of-the-way places. Families kept their dogs at home so they wouldn't be abducted and sold.

139 » Eat yeot!

Yeot meokeora! 엿 먹어라!

Screw you! Once a kid's favorite, yeot is a sticky candy made of rice and fermented barley. A peddler meandered through a village, yelling "Buy yeot!" Children begged their mothers to buy them the candy. If that didn't work, the boldest pilfered bronze kitchen utensils and even their grandfather's rickety radio set and traded them for yeot. More than one boy traded the family dog for yeot. Hence the expression, "Where is your pride? Did you trade it for yeot?"

Yeot sticks to hands, and hair becomes a horrible tangle if it brushes against the stuff. Thus Koreans associate yeot with embarrassment, but it also has positive symbolism. Parents attach globs of it to the gate of the school where their children take college entrance exams, hoping it will glue their offspring to a prestigious university. Relatives and friends present exam-takers with sticks of yeot.

Meorie pido an mareun nom 머리에 피도 안 마른 놈

140 » The blood has hardly dried on his head.

He should grow up. Older people refer to upstarts with this contemptuous phrase, which recalls a baby that has just been born. Similar put-downs:

"He still reeks of milk."

"Hair has yet to grow on his head."

"He wants to run when he can't even crawl."

Confucian values stress respect for seniority. Fathers reign over their families, although women are now much more assertive than they used to be. Outside the home, respect for seniority is losing ground. A decade ago, youngsters shot up from their bus or subway seats and gave their spots to the elderly. If they didn't, brassy old men gave them a tongue-lashing: "Don't you have a father at home?" Today, subway cars have seats reserved for old passengers, but many young people occupy them and pretend to sleep.

MORE TOUGH TALK

- "Is that thing you're carrying up there a head?"
- "Is this the first time you've seen a human being?" Or "I will gouge your eyes out."

Why are you looking at me like that, moron?

- "I will soak you in water, take you out and beat you until dust rises from your body."
- "I will crack open that watermelon of a head you've got."
- "You act as if you had several throats."

I will cut your throat.

- "Stop splitting your face!"

Quit smiling.

- "I will make sashimi out of you."

For the maximum effect, say this while brandishing a long knife.

- "Did you rent this place?"

Move your fat lump and make room for me.

- "She acted like a crazy woman playing a seesaw."

She was out of control. During the lunar New Year's Day, young village women played "plank-jumping," a traditional game in which they stood on the ends of a seesaw and jumped higher and higher. During the autumn Full Moon Harvest Day, they rode swings tied to a big tree. In both games, women wore colorful, flowing dresses that caught the wind and billowed with each jump or swing. In Korean slang, there are more references to the behavior of crazy women than mad men. Such expressions are fading.

Seongeul galgetda 성을 갈겠다

141 » I swear I'll change my family name.

People say this to stress a point. "It's true! If not, I swear I'll ...." In South Korea, changing a family name is illegal. It's a taboo in a society that emphasizes ancestral worship and the perpetuation of the male family name.

"Dig your name out of my family lineage book and get out!" an angry father says to a child.

By law, children must maintain their father's family names. This practice creates an awkward situation for children of a divorced couple. In most divorce arrangements, children live with their mothers because mothers are expected to look after children. But they can't adopt their stepfather's family name, exposing them to ridicule from classmates.

Yeol oreunda 열 오른다

142 » My body temperature is rising.

I'm about to blow my stack. Koreans also say: "My lid is about to blow off." Or "My blood is flowing backward." If you have to restrain yourself from slugging someone, say: "My fists are crying"(in frustration).

143 » You disgusting worm!

Beoreoji gateunnom! 버러지 같은 놈

This insult was on everyone's lips in 1979 when South Korea's intelligence chief, Kim Jae-gyu, killed President Park Chung-hee during a drinking party. Before gunning down Park, Kim fatally shot chief presidential bodyguard Cha Ji-chul, calling him a "disgusting worm." Kim was later executed.

Park, a former school teacher and Japanese colonial army lieutenant, took power in a military coup in 1961. He often wore black sunglasses, which were called 'laibang,' a distorted pronunciation of the brand-name Ray-Ban. Sunglasses were also "MacArthur glasses," named after the American general, Douglas MacArthur, who led U.S. forces in 1950-51 during the Korean War. They were once a fad among South Korean marines who couldn't resist striking a pose like MacArthur on the day of his victorious amphibious landing at Incheon, a western port near Seoul.

Park, a no-nonsense leader, marshaled the country into high-speed economic growth. But he suppressed political dissent and human rights to prolong his rule. His assassination came shortly after thousands of students launched pro-democracy protests.

144 » I wish to kill him and then dig up and dismember his body.

Many Korean insults originate in old execution methods. If a criminal was deemed to deserve a greater punishment than death, his body was exhumed after execution and his head and limbs were chopped off. Royal courts did this to dead court ministers if it was later learned that they had plotted sedition or committed other serious crimes. The measure was severe because it was taboo to tamper with the remains of the dead.

A despotic Yi Dynasty king, Yon San Kun, ordered the remains of many court ministers to be dug up and defiled because he suspected them in the death of his mother.

His mother was "Yoon the Deposed Queen," a wife of King Sung Jong. Court ministers bickered with her, and she was banished from the palace. The king sent her a bowl of poison and ordered her to commit suicide. Yoon drank the potion, and threw up blood onto a patch of hemp cloth that she passed to her mother. Yoon's dying wish was that her son, Yon San Kun, see the cloth and learn of her fate. He eventually did after coming to the throne, and went berserk.

Yon San Kun massacred more than 100 court officials and scholars in 1504, accusing them of plotting against his mother. The remains of long-buried ministers were disgraced in public. The king banned the teaching of the Korean alphabet, created only a few decades earlier, and ordered the burning of all Korean textbooks after posters criticizing his bloodlust were discovered in Seoul. He was incensed because the posters were written in the new alphabet.

After a decade in power, Yon San Kun was dethroned in a coup.

Jurireul teul nom/nyeon 주리를 틀 놈/년

145 » He/she should be tortured.

Juri was the most common tool for torturing criminals in old Korea. Authorities strapped a criminal to a chair and placed two rods between her legs. Two men pressed down on the rods on both sides of the victim, breaking or dislocating leg bones. The goal was to extract confessions. In the 19th century, authorities used it to force Catholic converts to disavow their religion.

Numerous pro-democracy activists of the 1970s and 1980s said torture was rampant during interrogations.

"The torture master," or police Captain Lee Kun-an, was a name they all remembered with dread. Lee's favorite techniques were dislocating arms and legs, jolting his victims with high-voltage electricity and pouring pepper-laced water into their noses. Many political prisoners said they were convicted of being communist spies and sentenced to prison terms on the basis of false confessions extracted by Lee. Governments decorated him 16 times for his service, but he went into hiding in 1988 after political prisoners were released and accused him of torture. He was the country's most wanted criminal suspect until he surrendered in 1999 and was sentenced to seven years in prison.

Lee said he lived behind a stack of carton boxes at his house when he was a fugitive, writing books on the Bible that he never published.

Yuksihal nom 육시할 놈

146 》 Somebody should kill him by tearing his body into six pieces.

The condemned man's head and limbs were tied to five carts, and executioners whipped horses pulling the carts in different directions. This was a punishment for sedition or parricide in old Korea.

Sayak, or a poison bowl from the king, was used when the criminals were royal relatives and court ministers. Those who lost a power struggle were liable to be accused of sedition and exiled.

"You traitor! Come out and receive sayak!" the chief executioner bellowed as his soldiers barged into the exile's house. The condemned knelt before the bowl. Some records say they were first required to make a farewell bow in the direction of Seoul before drinking the poison.

147» They should boil him alive. Yukjangnael nom 육장낼 놈

A fate reserved for corrupt government officials, though historical records show that the criminal was not actually boiled. In Seoul, the punishment was often conducted in front of a big crowd in Chongno, a downtown thoroughfare. Authorities stacked firewood under a large cauldron filled with lukewarm water, and the criminal was led out and thrown into the cauldron. But the kindling was never lit. The criminal's family, clad in funeral costumes, wailed over the mock execution. They later took the man home in a simulated funeral procession. The public episode was a great humiliation for the family, and the man could not leave his home and was effectively banished from society.

Chongno is now a commercial center full of neon lights, music blaring from storefronts, youngsters chattering on cellphones and demonstrators carrying placards and shouting slogans.

7 Money Talks

From olden times, Koreans were captivated by the power of money. But they also advised frugality and measures against corruption.

148 》 One must look upon gold as stone.

Resist temptation. This anti-corruption maxim is often attributed to Choi Young, a stubborn, idealistic general of the 14th-century Koryo Dynasty who made his name fighting Japanese bandits. He persuaded his king, Woo, to mobilize a large expedition to reclaim the land Korea once held in Manchuria but had lost to the Chinese. Critics thought it reckless to fight China's powerful Ming Dynasty, which considered Korea a client kingdom. Such a campaign would have entailed moving large forces in monsoon season, leaving Korea's southern flank vulnerable to Japan.

The leader of these critics was General Yi Sung-ke, Choi's rival. King Woo and Choi dismissed the criticism, so Yi feigned to oblige and led the expedition. When the army reached the Yalu River on the border with China, Yi turned it around.

"If I cross this border, I will be guilty before the 'Son of Heaven' (Chinese king) and great hardship will befall my nation and people," Yi said.

Yi returned to the capital, killed both King Woo and Choi, and replaced the Koryo with the Yi Dynasty.

Some historians lament that the moment Yi turned his army around symbolized the end of Korea's northern-bound expansion, and the birth of *sadae*, or submission to foreign powers. Generations of Yi Dynasty kings and leaders of modern Korea have been accused of *sadae*. But other historians say Yi's decisive action was a wise course for a nation whose destiny remains intertwined with its bigger neighbors.

Kkekkeuthagiga Hwang Hee jeongseung 깨끗하기가 황희 정승

149 》 He is as honest as Minister Hwang.

Hwang Hee, a Yi Dynasty court minister, never took bribes even though his family was so poor that his wife and daughters had to share their only good skirt for outings. He posted a roll of silk and a dead chicken, along with the names of the donors of these bribes, at the gate of his house. The bribes rotted there for years and served as a warning to any visitor tempted to try the same tactic.

According to historical records, the houses of influential royal court ministers attracted long lines of people hoping to buy jobs or favors with gifts.

There is a story about two friends who vowed to each other that they would never resort to bribery to get a government job. After many years, they were still unemployed, so one buckled and visited a Cabinet minister's house with a bribe. He arrived early in the morning so others wouldn't see him. Ushered into the anteroom, he saw another man already waiting for the minister to wake up. It was his friend.

Donimyeon cheonyeo buraldo sanda 돈이면 처녀 불알도 산다

150》 Money can buy the testicles of a virgin.

Anything is possible with money.

"You can even hire a ghost with money."

"With money, a dog can become a barking government official." A stupid, yet rich man can buy his way into a government post.

"Your appetite returns just when you have run out of money." Money is scarce when you most need it.

"You sit when you lend money, but you stand when you collect it." Lending is easy, but collecting a debt isn't.

Koreans are upfront about money. They want to know how much a friend paid for a new car or piece of clothing. They go to funerals and weddings with cash envelopes. Sitting at a desk, the receptionist collects the envelopes, counts the bills and logs the amounts and donors' names in a ledger – sometimes while the donors are still standing there.

The noble yangban class of old made a show of treating money as dirty and dangerous. They considered it a taboo to touch money with bare hands, and used chopsticks and dishes or wore gloves to handle it.

Teoleoseo meonji an naneun nom eopda 털어서 먼지 안 나는 놈 없다

151 » Dust rises from everybody when they're thrashed.

Every closet has a skeleton. This is often a veiled threat: I know you are not as clean as you pretend to be, and we will find your dirty laundry.

Chonji 촌지

152 » Small, humble expression of gratitude, the size of a finger joint.

It used to mean a small gift, offered in thanks. Today it means an envelope stuffed with bills, which epitomizes the culture of cash gifts in South Korea. The entrenched system sometimes serves as a front for bribery. The anti-corruption campaigns of successive governments have had some success, though the problem persists.

THE 'ENVELOPE' CULTURE

Some Koreans regard small cash gifts as a natural gesture, much like tipping in a restaurant or greeting with a bow. Cash gifts called *tteokgap*, or "rice cake expenses," are distributed during major holidays, supposedly to help the recipient cover vacation expenses. Rice cake is a traditional holiday food.

"Appreciation money" (*saryebi*) is paid when a request is met and a case resolved, or whitewashed.

Usually, the money flows upward. When the current is reversed, it's "encouragement money" (*gyeoklyeokum*), a gentle slap on the back in the form of a cash envelope. A person transferring to a new job gets "farewell money" (*jeonbyeolkum*). A client going on an overseas trip takes "horse coach money" (*kirmabi*), supposedly to help cover travel expenses.

The gifts are a way of saying thanks, but sometimes a favor is expected in return. "It was just rice cake money!" protest those accused of bribery. In that case, Koreans like to cite the classic denial of a cow thief: "I never stole the cow. I just picked up a rope on the street and took it home. I had no idea that a cow was attached to the rope."

There is also *jeopdae*, or "reception," during which whiskey flows and "food is stacked so heavily that the table legs warp." The session takes place in expensive restaurants or cloistered bar rooms attended by hostesses.

Old Koreans called bribes "bird feed" or "rat feed." Birds and rats stole grain from government granaries filled with rice collected as taxes.

Journalists stumbling onto corruption are sometimes offered hush money from those who want to "gag their mouths"(*ipmak yi*). Prosecutors occasionally arrest journalists on charges of taking money with threats to expose corruption or with promises to do favorable stories.

For most people, the cash gift is known just as *bongtu*, or the "envelope."

Bribing traffic police is not as common as it once was. But parents still provide school teachers with envelopes containing cash or gift certificates. Some parents fear teachers will mistreat their children if they don't give gifts. Many teachers turn them down.

Some politicians and big businessmen dealt in briefcases, which Koreans call "007 bags," named after James Bond.

In 1997, an aide to President Kim Young-sam was jailed for collecting bribes from businessmen. The man, Hong In-gill, coined a phrase that outlived his career.

"I am just a feather" (*gitteol*), he said, meaning he was a minor-league player in the Great Corruption Bazaar. Seoul's rumor mill got busy, with newspapers speculating who was *mom-tong*, or "main body." Bribery scandals also rocked the government of President Kim Dae-jung.

The envelope is a fixture of weddings and funerals. The original idea was to chip in to help friends defray expenses. But turnout at such events has become a yardstick of social standing, so families invite as many guests as possible. They invite distant kinsfolk, business acquaintances, long-lost classmates and army buddies. Governments urged the public to invite only close friends and relatives, and to reject wreaths or cash donations to cut down on lavish spending. Few heeded.

Gaecheoreom beoleo jeoseucheoreom sseora 개처럼 벌어 정승처럼 써라

153 » You should earn your money like a dog, but spend it like a royal court minister.

Work long hours at lowly jobs if you must, but spend your savings on a noble cause.

Newspapers revived this old saying in the late 1990s in honor of Yoo Yang-sun, an old widow who sold anchovy sauce seven days a week in a market stall. She donated her fortune to schools to help pay tuition for needy students. When reporters visited her tiny apartment, they found a 20-year-old refrigerator, a three-year-old toothbrush, and over 1,000 letters from students she had supported.

The expression also applies to Kim Young-han, who was a teen-ager when she became a "kisaeng," a female dancer of low social status. She fell in love with a famous poet, Baek Suk. The two were separated when the man returned to his hometown in North Korea and the Korean War broke out.

Kim stayed in Seoul and became owner of Dae Won Gak, South Korea's best-known traditional restaurant and "kisaeng house." Numerous politicians frequented her establishment to engage in what people call "secret-room politics" and "kisaeng-house politics."

Before she died in 1999 at age 83, Kim created a literary award in the name of her former lover and donated the premises of Dae Won Gak, worth $77 million, to a Buddhist denomination to turn it into a temple and Zen training center.

Ja Rin Ko Bi 자린고비

154 》 Mr. Ja Rin Ko Bi.

A frugal person. Ja Rin Ko Bi, a folk tale figure, was rich but so miserly that he never ate meat or fish. Instead, he dangled a dried fish on a string from the ceiling and gazed at it as he spooned down his gruel, savoring the fish in his imagination. In the summer, he held his fan taut so as not to wear it out and shook his head left and right to make a breeze.

Ja Rin Ko Bi originally meant "miser." After the Korean War, the government often cited Ja Rin Ko Bi while exhorting people to save in order to help rebuild the shattered economy. In those days, all schoolchildren were encouraged to have their own bank accounts to save what little they had, and the youngest kept coins in piggy banks. Banks diverted private savings to finance manufacturing industries. Today, the government no longer emphasizes savings as the economy is fueled by household consumption as well as exports.

Yeolgil ttangeul pado don hanpun an naonda 열길 땅을 파도 돈 한 푼 안 나온다

155 》 Even if you dig ten fathoms underground, you won't find a single coin.

Money doesn't grow on trees. There are no shortcuts in life.

The saying upholds the merits of cutting waste and saving. Old Koreans regard gold items as a saving for times of great duress like the Korean War. Gold in the shape of keys and turtles, symbols of good luck and long life, are common gifts for friends and relatives on important anniversaries. Families present newborn babies with gold rings.

During the 1997-98 Asian financial crisis, millions of South Koreans swarmed into banks to sell 222 tons of rings, necklaces and other gold trinkets worth 2.22 billion dollars in a nationwide "gold drive" to help their country earn hard currency to pay foreign debts. Most of the gold was melted into ingots and exported for dollars.

The gold drive originated in a 1907 campaign launched by a dozen civilian leaders to help pay back national debts owed to Japan, which was soon to colonize Korea. People donated money, gold and other jewelry until the Japanese sabotaged the campaign by arresting its leaders on embezzlement charges. Japan used debts as a means of ensuring Korea's economic dependency until it annexed the country in 1910.

8 From Elsewhere

Koreans borrowed terms from Japanese and English,
sometimes giving them new meanings.
But Chinese retains the deepest influence over
the Korean language.

156 » Italy towel.

Italy towel 이태리 타월

It's unclear how "Italy" became a part of this English-language term. In South Korea, you go to your bathtub with an "Italy towel." It's a coarse, palm-sized cloth. You soak yourself in the hot water and scrape your body vigorously with the "Italy towel" to remove grime. In a public bathhouse, you ask the person sitting next to you to rub your back with the towel, and you return the favor. The towelette is such a necessity for Koreans that tour guidebooks tell people going abroad not to forget it.

157 » Turkish bathhouse.

Turkey tang 터키탕

A bathhouse that commonly served as a front for a brothel, offering "comfortable massages." Similar establishments in Japan were also called "Turkish bathhouses" until the mid-1980s, when most changed their names to "soapland" following protests by Turkish and Middle Eastern residents.

In 1996, the Turkish embassy protested the South Korean term, declaring it an insulting misnomer. The government cracked down on prostitution in those establishments and ordered them to change their names to "steam bathhouses." People still use the old term, although no longer on signposts.

158 » Sakura. Sakura 사쿠라

A Japanese term common in Korea. "Sakura" in Japanese means cherry blossom, the national flower of Japan.

In Korea, "sakura" means a shifty character, especially a politician who helps his party's rivals by secretly voting against his comrades. Note that Koreans give an unsavory meaning to the national flower of Japan.

During Japanese colonial rule, Koreans were banned from using their Korean names and language at school and in official documents. As a result, some Japanese terms slipped into the Korean language.

Anti-Japanese sentiments run deep among older Koreans. Such feelings are evident among youths as well, although they are readier to brush off history and embrace Japanese pop culture and electronics.

Koreans first adopted "sakura" to describe Koreans who collaborated with Japanese colonialists. "Sakura" also means "fake."

159 » No. 18. Sippalbeon 십팔번

Your favorite song. "What's your No. 18?" means, "What's the song you sing best?"

The phrase originated in Japan, where kabuki opera

performers demonstrate their best skills in the 18th act, the climactic scene.

160 » Death caused by too much work. Kwarosa 과로사

Called "karoshi" in Japan, this term was adopted by doctors and news media to describe the sudden death of office workers who suffered fatigue.

Korean companies traditionally took loyalty and long hours from their workers for granted, partly because it was hard to change jobs in the rigid labor market. In return, workers expected their company to provide lifetime employment. They still work long hours, six days a week, spending more time at the office than with their families. They attend "group dinners" with colleagues, followed by drinking and karaoke sessions. Office culture stresses conformity and all workers are expected to join.

Barely sober, workers wake early the next morning, navigate through maddening traffic jams and report to work to face their bosses, who drive them for more sales, new contracts and speedier paper-pushing. When the pressure lets up, some slip away to catch up on sleep in public bathhouses called "Sauna" that have a large room with rows of couches where naked office workers take a nap.

If some succumb to stress and fatigue and die, colleagues

lament the death as *kwarosa*.

Today, loyalty to the company is not as pronounced. Workers jump at chances for better pay elsewhere, and go to the gym or pursue other leisure activities after leaving the office.

Working conditions have improved vastly in the past two decades. In 1970, 22-year-old Chun Tae-il was one of thousands of young Koreans who toiled 14 to 16 hours a day in textile sweatshops where the ceiling was so low that workers had to stoop when moving. He tried to organize a labor union, but was stymied by police and employers. At a protest rally, Chun doused himself with gasoline and struck a match.

"We are not machines!" he shouted.

His self-immolation highlighted workers' hardship during South Korea's headlong industrialization, which was fueled by cheap labor, long working hours and collusion between authoritarian governments and family-controlled conglomerates.

Chun's death inspired thousands of college students to leave school and help organize labor unions in the 1980s. Authorities ferreted out these "employees in disguise" for punishment. Today, Chun is a legend among labor activists. A street at Seoul's Peace Market, where Chun worked, is named after him. The area is now filled with gleaming shopping towers open 24 hours a day, packed with young, affluent shoppers.

161 》 White Day.

White Day 화이트 데이

On Valentine's Day, South Korean and Japanese women give chocolates or red roses to the men they love. On March 14 – "White Day" – men return the sentiment with gifts. A popular theory of how "White Day" came to be: when young Japanese couples began celebrating romantic love on Valentine's Day in the 1970s, the confectionery industry boosted chocolate sales by making March 14 the day when men would reciprocate. On "White Day," the theory goes, you buy white chocolates for your beloved.

162 》 Western iron.

Yangcheol 양철

Tin plate or galvanized iron. When South Koreans had no ready terms for new items from abroad, they often attached *yang* (Western) to existing terms to create new names.

Hence *yangdongyi* ("Western urn" - metal pail or bucket), *yangeun* ("Western silver" - nickel), *yangbok* ("Western clothes" - suits), and *yangpa* ("Western leek" - onion).

163 » Puncture. Ppangkku 빵꾸

Ppangkku was the way Koreans pronounced the English "puncture."

Some say the mangled pronunciation was borrowed from the Japanese. *Ppangkku* now means a flat tire. It also means the act of scuttling a project, or failure to show up for a performance or appointment.

164 » Tin can. Kkangtong 깡통

An empty head with a big mouth. Most Koreans first saw tin cans when droves of American troops arrived for the Korean War. They began pronouncing "can" as *kkang*. *Tong* means container in Korean. People put the two terms together. War refugees used empty U.S. military cans to draw water, cook and beg for food. Empty cans became makeshift soccer balls for children. By and by, *kkangtong* came to mean a blabbering blockhead.

165 » Tantara. Ttanttara 딴따라

Derogatory slang for musicians, singers or other entertainers. Koreans adopted this onomatopoeic English word for the blare of a trumpet to describe an itinerant circus troupe's clowns and horn-blowers who paraded through villages to advertise evening shows.

Traditional Korean society highly regarded scholars but looked down on entertainers, who belonged to a low social class.

Today, pop singers and TV actors have huge fan clubs. Wealthy parents encourage their children to seek music and dancing careers. They buy children expensive instruments, hire tutors and even enroll them in overseas music schools.

Some families stick to the old way. When a son comes home with a funky hair style and declares that he wants to become a pop singer, the father may yell, "Why do you want to become a tantara?" Or he could – as young Koreans like to say about their conservative fathers – "fall on his back, biting bubbles in his mouth."

KONGLISH

The English language is creeping quirkily into Korean slang. When South Korea industrialized and English words flooded in, people couldn't find – or bother to find – proper translations. They chopped, patched or twisted English words to create wacky terms. Sometimes they adopted English words but gave them different uses and meanings. "Tantara" is an example.

This hybrid lingo is "Konglish."

A standup comedian is a "gagman," and people go "eye-shopping" to see what's on sale in department stores. "Quick Service men," or couriers, ride "autobis," or motorbikes.

A "villa" is an apartment building of just a few stories. A "venture company" could be an Internet-based firm, or any small start-up business. People shout "One shot!" when they propose a toast. A TV actor, talented or not, is a "talent." "Leports" combines leisure and sports.

The study of English is mandatory in schools from third grade through freshman year in university. But the stress has always been on reading and rote memorization of English grammar and vocabulary, rather than conversation. Many college graduates read complex textbooks in English, but freeze up in conversation. Schools are trying to reverse the lapse with more language labs, aware that economic competitiveness depends in part on mastery of the international language of business.

Before they invented their own alphabet in the mid-15th century, Koreans borrowed Chinese characters to write down their speech and coin new words. Chinese influence on Korean remains deep, despite the efforts of a handful of language purists to drive out foreign words.

The purists have a bigger say in North Korea, which creates Korean words for modern products. South Koreans say "ice cream" in English; in the North, it's "ice cotton balls" in Korean. The South uses the English word "dry-cleaning." Northerners say "chemical laundry" in their native tongue. The South is fine with the English word "helicopter;" North Koreans translate it as a "vehicle that takes off and goes straight up."

Mosun 모순

166 » Spear and shield.

A contradictory statement or development. A Chinese man sold his spears and shields at a market place. He said his spears could break any shields, and his shields could block any spears. A bystander quipped: "Why don't you try breaking your shield with your spear?"

Tosagupaeng 토사구팽

167 » When the rabbit is caught, the hunter kills, boils and eats his hunting dog.

Subordinates are expendable. This Chinese proverb came to prominence after Kim Jae-soon, a veteran politician and former National Assembly speaker, compared himself to a hunting dog in 1993. He helped Kim Young-sam get elected president in 1992, but was one of the first victims of the president's anti-corruption campaign. Kim Jae-soon was accused of amassing huge properties through dubious means. Kim denied any wrongdoing, and he was not prosecuted. But his image was in tatters, and he retired from politics. People called him "*sibeom* case," the combination of the Korean *sibeom*, or "demonstration," and the English "case." The slang means a scapegoat, especially one sacrificed as a warning to others.

168 » Nangpae.

Nangpae 낭패

Deadlock. In Chinese mythology, *nang* was a wolf-like animal without hind legs or with unusually short hind legs. *Pae* was born without front legs or had very short front legs. The two beasts could not move or hunt without each other. *Nang* was fierce but dumb, while *pae* was wise but timid. They quarreled whenever they hunted, and seldom caught any prey. They were destined to work together but nothing worked between them.

169 » Gyohwal.

Gyohwal 교활

Shrewd and vicious. *Gyo* is a mythic Chinese beast that looked like a dog but had leopard spots and bull horns. Its howls heralded a good harvest. Its friend, *hwal*, had a human-like body with a pig's hide, and hibernated in a cave. Its howls, which sounded like an axe striking a tree, signaled a crisis. Both beasts were ferocious and shrewd. When they saw a tiger, they rolled themselves into balls, jumped into the tiger's bowels and ate it from the inside out. Then they chuckled. Today, a malicious laugh is called the "giggle of *Gyohwal.*"

Bulhok 불혹

170 » The age of not succumbing to temptations.

Forty years old. Instead of saying he's turned 40, a Korean may say he is at the age of *bulhok*. The expression is attributed to Confucius, who said: "At 15, I wanted to study. At 30, I became independent. At 40, I could repel temptations. At 50, I realized the mission that Heaven gave me. At 60, I could easily understand what other people said. At 70, I did whatever I pleased, but none of my deeds broke any law."

Yuye 유예

171 » Yuye.

Delay. Hesitation. *Yu* was a monkey-like animal in Chinese legend. It was so cautious that it jumped onto a tree at the slightest noise. *Ye* was a mammoth-like animal so indecisive that it spent all its life beside a stream, afraid that underwater beasts would attack it if it tried to cross. It put one foot in the water and then retreated, repeating the ritual forever.

Samsipyukgye 삼십육계

172 » 36th Strategy.

Run away! Ancient Chinese generals had 36 war strategies. The last says, "running away is the best thing to do when the enemy is overwhelming."

A few others:

● "Use a borrowed sword to attack your enemy."

Let your allies attack your enemy.

● "Observe the fire across the river."

From a safe distance, wait for your enemy to disintegrate in internal discord.

● "Find a corpse to house a spirit."

A shrewd Chinese general promoted a figurehead king as a rallying point for the public and won the war against his rivals. The king had been a spent force, but the general found a use for him.

● "Look at the cicada slipping out of its shell."

Retreat while making your enemy believe that you are still in a fighting position. Leave effigies of soldiers in your old positions, just as the cicada sheds its skin, and then attack the enemy's unguarded flanks.

● "Point your finger at the mulberry tree and scold the locust tree."

Attack a lesser enemy to warn a bigger rival.

● "Put fake flowers on a tree."

Make your military look bigger and better-armed than it really is.

173 » A long-snake deployment. Jangsajin 장사진

A long line of people waiting to buy tickets or enter a concert hall. In an old Chinese military tactic, troops were deployed in a long line over the terrain. When the enemy attacked the "head" of the snake deployment, "the tail" made a circling maneuver to assault the enemy from behind.

Baesujin, or "deploying troops with a river behind them," forces soldiers to fight fiercely because they have nowhere to run. "This is our last chance to advance to the second round. We must fight with a river behind our back," sports commentators say.

174 » Gi. gi 기

Gi is the energy believed to flow through a human body. It's different from physical strength, which is called *him*.

"He has a strong gi." He has mental strength, tenacity or stubbornness.

"His gi is dead/drained." He is crestfallen or humiliated.

"My gi was blocked/bottlenecked." I was dumbfounded or outraged.

When military commanders order sloppy soldiers to do push-ups, they call it *gihap*, or "putting gi back together."

175 Broken mirror.

Pakyeong 파경

Divorce. A Chinese man broke a mirror in half and gave one piece to his wife, who was abducted and sold as a slave by enemy troops. Many years later, the man identified his wife by putting together their halves of the broken mirror. Unlike its present meaning, the broken mirror used to symbolize the reunion of a couple.

"It's a broken mirror." No use crying over spilt milk.

176 My eyebrows are on fire.

Chomi 초미

People say this if a situation is desperate and requires a quick remedy.

177 Reading books by the tail light of fireflies and by the reflections of moonlight on snow.

Hyeongseoljigong 형설지공

Studying hard to pass an important exam, despite setbacks or obstacles. A poor Chinese man collected a bagful of fireflies to read his books. Korean parents cite this old Chinese expression in urging children to study hard.

178 » Chicken ribs.

Kyereuk 계륵

Something you don't want but can't throw away. Chicken ribs have little meat.

Gusuhoeui 구수회의

179 » Pigeons bringing their heads together in a meeting.

Executives at a brainstorming session reminded Chinese of pigeons gathering for feed.

180 » Worries of Mr. Gi.

Giwu 기우

Baseless anxiety. A man from ancient China's Gi Kingdom refused to walk outside his home because he feared the sky might fall on him or the ground might cave in under his feet.

Dangranggeocheol 당랑거철

181 » A praying mantis challenging the rolling wheel of a horse-drawn cart.

Bluster that will only lead to self-ruin. A Chinese king saw a praying mantis standing before his carriage, wielding its axe-like front legs as though ready to fight.

"If it were a man, it would make a great general. I wish my

generals were as brave as the bug," said the king, ordering his driver to turn the vehicle to make way for the insect.

Today, the phrase more often refers to bravado than boldness.

182 » White eyebrows. Baekmi 백미

A genius. A masterpiece. A Chinese couple had five talented sons. The one with white eyebrows, Baek Mi, was the best and became a Cabinet minister.

Baek Mi's brother, Ma Sok, was a young general. When he failed to keep his promise to defend a hill to the death, his commander was obliged to execute him. The commander wept because he loved the young general but had to honor the regulations. Today, when a scandal forces Korean leaders to fire a trusted aide, they call it *eupchammasok*, or "beheading Ma Sok while crying."

183 » Sheep's head and dog's meat. Yangduguyuk 양두구육

False advertisement. Counterfeit. A butcher hangs a sheep's head outside his shop but sells dog meat disguised as mutton. Koreans rarely consume mutton, but this Chinese phrase is widespread.

Yangsanggunja 양상군자

184 » The gentleman on the crossbeam.

A thief or rat. In old China and Korea, these nocturnal creatures crept along the crossbeam of the house.

Osipbo baekbo 오십보 백보

185 » A man who fled 50 feet calls a man who fled 100 feet a coward.

Don't laugh at me. You are no better.

Ohapjijol 오합지졸

186 » Troops like a flock of ravens.

A ragtag army. Ravens fight each other over a carcass. If one throws a stone at the flock, the birds flee in all directions.

Bukmangsan gada 북망산 가다

187 » Go to Bukmang Mountain.

Die. Bukmang Mountain is a hill near Luoyang, an ancient Chinese capital in the Henan Province. The mountain was famous for its many tombs of kings and other dignitaries. In Korea, the mountain has become a synonym for the abode for the dead.

Samyeonchoga 사면초가

188 » Hometown songs from all four directions.

A hopeless situation. This phrase recalls Hang Woo, a great Chinese warlord whose name today is a synonym for a strong man.

Enemy forces surrounded Hang Woo's camp and forced captured soldiers to sing their hometown songs, weakening the morale of the besieged troops. Hang Woo eventually broke through enemy lines and reached a river where a boat was waiting for him. The general let his beloved horse, Choo, and his remaining troops cross the river to safety. But he remained and fought alone, killing hundreds of enemy soldiers before his demise, according to the legend. His deed is often cited as a classic case of a failed leader who kept his dignity.

Eobujiri 어부지리

189 » It will only benefit the fisherman.

A windfall. A situation where a third party benefits from a quarrel between two rivals.

In a Chinese fable, a snipe tried to pick the insides of a sunbathing clam. The clam snapped its shell shut on the bird's beak.

"If you don't let me go, you will dry out and die," the bird said.

"I don't care. If I don't let you go, you will starve to

death," the clam said.

Neither backed down. A passing fisherman easily caught the clam and the bird.

Daegimanseong 대기만성

190 » It takes a long time to craft a great piece of pottery.

This saying extols perseverance. It also refers to a person of humble origin who becomes a high-ranking government official late in his career, or a young person of little talent who becomes a master in old age. Some families hang a framed copy of this adage on the living room wall. Another inspirational message for the home: "When you have a happy family, everything will turn out well for you."

The pottery aphorism derives from the work of Lao-tzu, the Chinese founder of Taoism.

Saeongjima 새옹지마

191 » Everything in life is like an old man's horse.

You don't know how your luck will change. The horse of an old Chinese man ran away, and his neighbors consoled him.

"Who knows? This could be a good sign for me," he said.

A few days later, the horse returned with another, stronger horse. The villagers congratulated the old man.

"You never know. This could turn out badly for me," he said.

A few days later, his only son broke his leg when he fell off the new horse. The villagers lamented the bad news.

"Don't feel sorry for me," the old man said. "This could be a lucky development."

Everybody thought the man was mad.

War broke out a few days later, and the government conscripted young villagers to the front lines. The old man's only son was exempt because of his broken leg. Most of the village's young men never returned from the war.

Gyeolchoboeun 결초보은

192 》 Returning an old favor by tying the weeds.

Never forgetting a favor. *Boeun*, or "repaying favors," is a common theme in Korean folk tales.

A rich Chinese man told his son that his concubine should be allowed to remarry when he died. On his deathbed, however, he lost his wits and ordered his son to bury the young woman alive with him. The grieving son disregarded the command and let the concubine remarry.

Years later, the son became a general and went to war. In a battle, he was fleeing enemy soldiers when he looked back and saw the enemy general's horse tumble.

The tide of the battle turned. The victor later learned that an old man had tied weeds into numerous traps that ensnared the hooves of enemy horses. In a dream that night, the old man told the general that he was repaying his debt because the general once saved his daughter, the concubine.

Wasinsangdam 와신상담

193 》 Sleeping on billets and licking at gallbladders.

Never forgetting to seek revenge. Determined to make a comeback. A Chinese king was defeated in a battle with a rival and died of his injuries. In his last moments, he asked his son to avenge his death. From then on, the son refused to sleep on his comfortable bed, choosing instead a pile of firewood. All aides entering his room were required to shout: "Don't forget who killed your father!"

The son defeated the rival king, but ignored his aides' advice to kill the enemy, and let him return home. The defeated king carried an animal gallbladder and licked it to remind himself of his bitter humiliation. After a dozen years, he rebuilt his army and attacked again, occupying the kingdom of his dead rival's son. In a reversal of fate, he offered to spare the son. But the mortified son rejected the offer and killed himself.

9
Slang and Seoul

With 10 million people and a vibrant youth culture, South Korea's capital is the ultimate incubator of modern expressions.

194 It kills me! Jukinda! 죽인다!

Koreans who say this are not referring to homicide, a case of food poisoning or some other calamity. Quite the contrary. This expression describes the good, absurd, funny, nonsensical, interesting or exceptional. People raving over a succulent meal say: "It kills me! What are the ingredients?"

When Koreans hear something absurd, they say: "I can't believe what he just said. Is he serious? It kills me!"

195 King of Bad Luck. Wangjaesu 왕재수

The king of jerks. *Wang* in Korean is "king." *Jaesu* means "good luck," but it means bad luck in this case. The term applies to someone you really don't like. You think the mere sight of him brings you bad luck.

Wanghoejang, or "the King Chairman," was the nickname for the late Chung Ju-yung, an obscure rice dealer who became the charismatic founder and chairman of the Hyundai conglomerate and symbolized South Korea's industrial leap.

Wangchobo, or "the king of novices," is a greenhorn. It's also a humorous sign you find on some rear windshields in Seoul's traffic jams. Impatient drivers switch lanes to get a few feet ahead. They honk and curse at drivers who move slowly or cut into their lanes. On rear windshields, some drivers tape signs saying, *wangchobo*, or *chobowunjeon* (which means a novice driver). The unwritten message: I just got my driver's license, so please don't harass me.

196 ## Wangtta.

Wangtta 왕따

A pariah. One ostracized from classmates or colleagues; or the act of ostracizing.

Popular among teenagers, this phrase combines *wang*, which is "king" or "main" in Korean, and the first Korean syllable of *ttadolrim*, which means "ostracism."

SCHOOL

Wangtta and bullying are problems – some would say an outgrowth – of South Korea's strict school system, in which pressure to succeed is enormous. Rote-learning for college entrance exams is such that high schools are referred to as "exam hell."

Some parents send children to "Survival Camp," where they scoot, crawl, run, rappel, do push-ups and chin-ups, and go through other routines modeled on those at marine boot camps. Marine sergeants yell as the kids run shirtless and shiver in a stream, singing military songs, on the coldest day of the year. Parents hope the training will help children adapt to pressure-cooker conditions at school.

Teachers of old were stern and unforgiving. Confucian ideas stressed that the "king, teacher and father are one and the same" (*gunsabuilche*). In old schools called *Seodang*, or "Houses of Letters," the teacher sat cross-legged on the floor, his hand occasionally sweeping his long beard. He wore a horsehair top hat, read dog-eared Confucian textbooks spread on a small table, and stared down at students with "tiger's eyes." Students knelt before the teacher and read their textbooks on the floor. Boys who failed to memorize poems and textbooks were summoned and told to roll up their trouser legs. The teacher's bamboo stick whistled through the air and landed on trembling calves. Other boys, waiting their turn, winced at every blow. Hence the expression, "If you have to be whipped, it's best to be whipped first."

These old schools were exclusively for boys. Families denied girls formal education until the early 20th century. Parents used to say: "Girls don't need education."

Until the early 1990s, the hickory was a common means of establishing classroom order. Teachers hit students if they were late, had a runny nose, pushed and shoved in line, or couldn't add or subtract.

Gyopyeon japda, or "picking up the educational rod," is the Korean expression for becoming a teacher. The paddle is euphemistically referred to as the "rod of love."

All Korean men remember a punishment called "Wonsan Bombardment." The victim put his head on the ground and then raised his hips, forming an arch with his body. Only his head and two feet touched the ground. His hands were locked behind his back. With the student poised in this painful position, a teacher sometimes whacked his buttocks with a rod. It was a common punishment in the South Korean military as well.

The name comes from heavy U.S. aerial attacks on Wonsan, a key beachhead on North Korea's east coast, during the Korean War. The student's head on the ground, with two spread legs, was supposed to resemble a U.S. plane nose-diving toward Wonsan.

Parents and children occasionally report bruises, burst eardrums and other injuries inflicted by teachers. The Education Ministry allows teachers to use corporal punishment only when it is "inevitable for educational purposes." It bans teachers from beating students with broom sticks, slippers, belts, rolled-up newspapers or attendance books.

Amid parental complaints, corporal punishment is disappearing from schools. Yet many parents pick up the hickory occasionally to keep kids in line at home.

Bapmatyida 밥맛이다

197» I lose my appetite whenever I see him.

I can't stand him. This expression is often shortened to *bapmat*, which means "appetite." If a girl calls you *bapmat*, she thinks you're a jerk.

Hwajangbal/Jomyeongbal 화장발/조명발

198» Cosmetics effect. Lighting effect.

When a woman slaps on too much makeup, her friends taunt her for seeking a "cosmetics effect." The implication is that she only looks good because of the cosmetics. "Is she a cosmetics effect or what?" is a snide comment among men and women.

To a man scanning the discotheque floor or bar, a woman dancing or sipping her drink under the lights could look alluring. Later, after the alcohol has worn off, the man may say, "She was just a lighting effect."

Plastic surgery is a booming industry in South Korea. Women flock to clinics to make their noses higher and their eyelids double-edged, pare down high cheekbones and remove wrinkles.

Showing romantic affection in public used to be a taboo. Today, young couples often kiss openly in bars. In some Seoul night clubs, sleek waiters arrange "bookings," on-the-spot setups between customers. They drag female customers by the wrist to tables of men, and many women go along with it.

Some older people seek their own "bookings" in "Cabaret" night clubs, which reverberate to the tune of slower Korean pop songs.

The relatively few who frequent these establishments seek clubs where "the water is good." That means the places are teeming with beautiful people.

199 》 I'm going to Hong Kong. HongKong ganda 홍콩 간다

I'm in heaven. One possible explanation for how Hong Kong entered Korean slang is that it has been a top shopping destination for South Koreans.

200 》 Cool! Siwonhada! 시원하다!

The term literally means cool, but it's also about what makes a Korean feel good. People say it when their team beats an archrival or when villains get their just deserts. In the latter case, people also say, "*Gosohada!*" This means: It tastes good!

After a hard day's work, a Korean downs a glass of beer and declares: "*Siwonhada!*" Reeling with hangovers, people go to restaurants for *haejangguk*, or pepper-laced "soup that unties your intestines," and declare: "Cool!" So do people who sip hot chocolate in winter or people who go to public bath-houses and take a dip in the large, communal bathtub.

201 » That's the carrot! Danggeunyiji! 당근이지!

Of course! Right on! A recent addition to youth jargon. Why "carrot"? One possible explanation is that "carrot" is *danggeun* in Korean. That sounds similar to *dangyeon*, which means "Of course."

Koreans believe carrots are the favorite food of a horse, and teenagers recently adopted a new slang term: "That's the horse feed!" (*malbapyiji*). It has the same meaning as "That's the carrot!"

202 » It's chilly. Sseolleonghada 썰렁하다

Give me a break. A boy tells a bad joke and guffaws. His friends roll their eyes and mutter: "It's chilly around here." Some say, "It's frosting up in here."

203 » I will shoulder the rifle. Chongdae meda 총대 메다

I'll take charge. Faced with a tough project, workers say, "So who's going to shoulder the rifle?" This expression probably refers to a soldier who shoulders his rifle and stands guard at night while the rest of the unit sleeps. All South Korean men serve 26 months in the military, a legacy of the long standoff with North Korea. Phrases with a military background have seeped into civilian talk.

204 》 I will shoot! Naega ssonda 내가 쏜다

Let's go out and party; food and drinks are on me. A term popular among young office workers. The implication is that money will fly out of the speaker's wallet like bullets.

205 》 I can hear your eyeballs rolling! Nunal gulrineun sori deulrinda 눈알 굴리는 소리 들린다

Silence! Don't move an inch! Drill sergeants in military boot camps shouted this at recruits on the parade ground. Other boot camp lines:

"I can't hear you, soldier! I want you to shout until your mom in your hometown hears you."

"Run! Run like a bullet!"

Drill sergeants gathered recruits after a hard day's training and told them to shout, "Mother! I will be a good son when I return home."

Some hated life in the military. Each day was tough. They

consoled themselves by saying: "The Defense Ministry's clock never stops ticking." In other words, it's only a matter of time before they get out of the military.

Gomusin bakkwe sineotda 고무신 바꿔 신었다

206 》 She changed her rubber shoes.

She found a new boyfriend. A dreaded expression for young men whose girlfriends abandon them while they are away from home, serving in the military.

The scenario of a man who finds a stranger's shoes in front of his wife's room inspired Korean scribes. The oldest example is a 9th century Shilla Kingdom poem, "The Song of Chir Yong." In the poem, the protagonist returns home on a moonlit night and finds four legs under his wife's quilt blanket. Chir Yong sings: "Two of them belong to me, but who is the owner of the other two?"

It was the God of Plagues disguised as Chir Yong. Instead of attacking the intruder, Chir Yong improvised a song and danced. Alarmed by this odd behavior, the evil god apologized and promised to never enter a house that hangs a portrait of Chir Yong. A Chir Yong talisman was common in Korea. People glued it on the crossbeam or on the wall over the living-room door.

207» My film stopped rolling.

Pilreum kkeungyeotda 필름 끊겼다

I passed out after heavy drinking. Koreans are seasoned drinkers who often liven up evenings with "bombs," or boilermakers. The fiery concoction of a shot glass of whiskey dumped into a brimming mug of beer was so ubiquitous in the 1980s that the Army Chief of Staff banned soldiers from drinking it. Today, office workers belt back boilermakers with a shout of "One shot!" Then they hold the mug high to prove that it's empty before passing it to the next drinker.

A few government officials have succumbed to scandals caused by slips of the tongue during drinking bouts. In 1999, one senior prosecutor swilled a few "bombs" with reporters. He boasted that he once helped trick labor activists into an illegal strike, giving the government an excuse to crack down on organized labor. Word got out, and the prosecutor and the justice minister lost their jobs.

"People speak their minds when drunk," Koreans say. The day after drinking, many Koreans pretend they don't remember a thing, saying: "My film stopping rolling at some point last night." That way, they dodge responsibility for their gaffes, such as retching in the lap of a colleague, making rude comments about their boss, or not picking up the tab as promised.

208 » He is blowing a trumpet.

Nabal bulda 나발 불다

He's ranting and raving. It more often means the act of downing alcohol in one gulp because a man with an upturned bottle in his mouth resembles a trumpet-blower.

Geu saram moreumyeon gancheopyida 그 사람 모르면 간첩이다

209 » You don't know him? You must be a communist spy.

He is so prominent that only a stranger wouldn't know him. To South Koreans, the ultimate stranger is a North Korean spy. Even today, concern about communist spies runs deep. In subway cars, signs urge people to report "suspicious characters" to authorities. Warning posters issued by the government's intelligence agency once depicted a wolf in a pulled-down hat and a long overcoat, a tail protruding from under its folds. Another showed a chameleon hiding among green leaves, with the caption: "If you look carefully, you can find him."

210 » An oppa legion.

Oppa budae 오빠 부대

A woman refers to her older brother as "oppa." Women also use the affectionate term for an older male friend. Cho Yongpil, a popular male singer in modern South Korea, had a throng of female fans who went wild at his pop concerts, chanting "Oppa!" People referred to his followers as the "oppa legion."

Now a man who is popular with women has his own "oppa legion." Cho, whose career peaked in the 1980s, was the first Korean singer to have a sustained following of raucous fans. Before he came along, concert fans were subdued because of Confucian emphasis on decorum and military governments that frowned on pop culture. In the 1970s, police armed with rulers stopped students in the streets, measuring boys' hair and girls' skirts in a drive against the spread of popular Western culture.

211 » She's a pumpkin. Hobak 호박

She's ugly. Men chuckle over this term out of earshot of the woman they are slandering. Young women coined a counter-punch: *poktan*, or "bomb." They mean that the man is so dirty, dangerous or unpredictable that you don't want to go near him: the bomb might explode.

212 » Yes, your wrist is thicker than mine! Ni palttuk gulda 니 팔뚝 굵다

Stop blowing your own horn! This sarcastic saying comes from the habit of small boys who bare their wrists to see which looks thickest and strongest.

Bihanggi taeuji mara 비행기 태우지 마라

213 » Don't give me a plane ride.

Stop flattering me.

Ppeong 뻥

214 » Ppeong.

An onomatopoeic word for the sound of a bursting balloon or tire. The Korean equivalent of the English "pop," "bang" or "boom." Popular among young Koreans, *ppeong* is also slang for a lie, exaggeration or joke. "Hey, that was *ppeong*, wasn't it?" people say when they think somebody is duping them.

Ppeong is also the name for a popcorn-like food made of rice. Roast rice in a high-pressure metal barrel. Unlock the lid, and pop – or *ppeong* – goes the rice. The "poprice" is much bigger than the original grain. Hence the analogy between *ppeong* and exaggeration. Poprice was food for lean days, a stomach filler.

ONOMATOPOEIC KOREAN WORDS

There are lots of onomatopoeic Korean words. Here is a selection:

- kung! (thud, thump) 쿵
- kwang! (a door slam) 쾅
- kko-kki-o (cock-a-doodle-do) 꼬끼오
- wing wing (buzz of a bee) 윙윙
- jjaek-kkak, jjaekh-kkak (tick-tock of a clock) 째깍째깍
- jjaek jjaek (tweet-tweet, the chirp of a bird) 짹짹
- ppi-yak ppi-yak (peep peep of a chick) 삐약삐약
- bu-geul bu-geul (the bubbling of boiling water) 부글부글
- wak-ja-ji-kkeol, or wa-geul wa-geul, or si-kkeul-beok-jeok (hubbub) 왁자지껄/와글와글/시끌벅적
- heol-le beol-tteok (hurly-burly of a hurrying, confused person) 헐레벌떡
- kang-kang, meong-meong (woof, bowwow of a dog) 캉캉, 멍멍
- kking kking (whine of a dog) 낑낑
- chik-chik pok-pok (choo choo, puff of a steam locomotive) 칙칙폭폭
- ppang ppang (honk honk of a car) 빵빵
- kul kul (snoring) 쿨쿨
- sae-geun, sae-geun (breathing of a sleeping baby) 새근새근
- kkul kkul (oink oink of a pig) 꿀꿀
- hu du du (pitter-patter of rain) 후두두

- dal-geu-rak, dal-geu-rak (clackety-clack of typewriter keys) 달그락달그락
- eong eong (boo-hoo of a weeping man) 엉엉
- nyam nyam (munch crunch) 냠냠
- bu-reung bu-reung (vroom of a car) 부릉부릉
- pi yung (zing, or whiz of an arrow or bullet) 피융
- ping (twang of a bow) 핑
- tu-deol, tu-deol (mutter, mumble of person) 투덜투덜
- dwing-gul dwing-gul (a rolling object, or a lazy man shifting his body on the floor) 뒹굴뒹굴
- cheom beong (splash of something falling into water) 첨벙
- du-geun, du-geun (the sound and feeling of a throbbing heart) 두근두근

Namjaneun yeoja hagi nareum 남자는 여자하기 나름

215 » A man's behavior depends on how the woman treats him.

This line from a 1990s television commercial for a washing machine found a place in street talk. It implies that a wife's traditional role is to treat her husband with the utmost respect, but it also suggests that women don't always fall into line. Some women turn the expression on its head: "A woman's behavior depends on how the man treats her."

The following is a sampling of one-liners from television

and print media advertisements that resonated with Koreans, helping the products sell well. They're not common in daily talk, but everybody remembers them.

"Sleep is your best medicine" - an old saying that found a new life in a bed commercial.

"We packed nothing but Thanks" - ad for gift sets.

"Wife is more beautiful than woman" - coffee cream. The subtext for men: don't go out on the town and succumb to temptation. Instead, go home early and have a cup of coffee with your wife. Don't forget. Use our cream.

"A wife who always looks like a lover" - cosmetics. The message: a wife should wear makeup to remain attractive to her husband.

"A woman like oxygen" - cosmetics. A woman who looks as fresh as clean air.

Hangange dol deonjigi 한강에 돌 던지기

216 » Throwing a stone into the Han River.

It won't make any difference. Also: "Urinating in the Han River." The Han River flows through Seoul.

Seouleseo kimseobang chatgi 서울에서 김서방 찾기

217 » That's like looking for a Mr. Kim in Seoul.

A needle in a hay stack. Twenty percent of South Korea's 47

million people have the same surname, Kim. The family name Lee is shared by 15 percent of the population, and Park by 8 percent.

Korea adopted a law in 1308 banning marriage between people with the same surname. At the time, inbreeding was a concern because people lived in isolated villages for generations. The ban conformed to Confucianism, which considered people with the same surname part of a single family no matter how many generations removed.

The ban had an enormous social impact because most Koreans share only a few dozen surnames. Tens of thousands of couples lived together but could not marry because they shared the same clan names, even though there was no evidence of blood ties. Once every few years, the government temporarily lifted the ban to let such couples marry.

In 1997, the Constitutional Court repealed the law. But marriage between people with the same surname remains a taboo.

Moro gado Seoulman gamyeondoeji 모로 가도 서울만 가면 되지

218» Even if you walk sideways, it's all right as long as you get to Seoul.

The end justifies the means.

SEOUL

An old saying: When a horse is born, send it to Jeju Island, home of South Korean horse-breeding; but send a newborn child to Seoul. Seoul became the capital of a unified Korea in 1394 when Yi Sung-ke, the founding king of the Yi Dynasty, moved his palace there from Songdo (Kesung in today's North Korea).

The city changed hands four times and was reduced to rubble during the Korean War. Seoul's population was 1 million at the end of the war. Now 17 million people – or just over a third of South Koreans – squeeze into Seoul or satellite cities that account for only 1.2 percent of the nation's total area.

The great Seoul job rush gained momentum with South Korea's economic growth in the late 1960s. Today, the capital attracts the nation's best jobs, best deals and best brains. Still, residents gripe about overpriced housing, pollution and bad manners.

Traffic is devilish in Seoul. Every day, 2,000 people get drivers' licenses, a tenfold increase from a decade ago. A total of 2.5 million cars are registered in the city and the number grows by several hundred each day. Accidents are frequent, and nearly 4,000 traffic tickets are handed out daily. Many violators are caught by freelance "hidden-camera men" who surreptitiously photograph license plates and report to police for 3,000 won ($ 2.3) per picture.

People crave space, hence all the signs advertising "rooms"

of every kind. There are "song rooms," "video rooms," "comic-book rooms," and even "sleeping rooms" where harried businessmen take a nap in cubbyholes. A saying advises constant alertness: "When you close your eyes in Seoul, they will cut your nose off." Or, "In Seoul, you may keep your eyes open and still have your nose cut off."

For all the hustle, Seoul people are friendly, upfront and kind to strangers. The streets are relatively safe. Modern subways take travelers to virtually any corner of the city. Seoul is surrounded by rocky mountains and on weekends, thousands of Seoulites head out for a day's climbing. On the mountain top, trekkers shout, "Ya Ho!"

10 Animal Kingdom

In the linguistic zoo of Korean,
a swallow dances and a loach becomes a dragon.
A host of animal characters spice up conversation.

DOG

219» Swallow. Jebi 제비

In folk tales, a swallow is a harbinger of good luck. Today, a "swallow" is a lowlife who loiters in night clubs and accosts women for a dance. The swallow's goal is to swindle money out of gullible victims, usually after having sex with them. The fop has mastered the dance steps and the art of sweet-talking, and usually drips with hair oil. He's a sharp dresser and resembles a swallow, whose long, parted tail reminds Koreans of a tuxedo.

220» Green frog. Cheonggaeguri 청개구리

A disobedient, unpredictable person. In a fable, the green frog never listened to his mother. When she told him to go east, he hopped west. When she ordered him to head south, he bounced north. On her deathbed, she told him, "Please bury me near the stream, not on the hill." She said this because she knew her son always did the opposite.

After his mother died, however, the green frog belatedly realized what a bad son he had been. He repented and did what his mother had requested, burying her near a stream. After that, the frog always worried that her grave would be swept away if it rained and the stream flooded. Even today, frogs croak woefully whenever it's about to rain.

Gaeguri olchaengyi jeok gieok mothanda 개구리 올챙이 적 기억 못한다

221 » The frog does not remember that it once was a tadpole.

An arrogant character who has forgotten his humble origins. Or, "The mother-in-law doesn't remember that she was once a daughter-in-law."

222 » A frog in a well.

Umul an gaeguri 우물 안 개구리

A narrow-minded person, ignorant of the outside world. Shut off from the rest of the world, Korea was known as the "hermit kingdom" until European and American traders, soldiers and missionaries – intrigued by talk of gold, new commercial frontiers and "pagans" in need of conversion to Christianity – came knocking in the late 19th century. Korea was one of the last Asian countries to open up.

Neighboring Japan outmaneuvered other powers and annexed the Korean peninsula in 1910. At the end of World War II, U.S. and Soviet forces divided Korea into the pro-Western South and the communist North. The South built an export-driven economy that evolved into one of the world's biggest. The North chose the opposite path. Today, it remains a starving "frog in the well," dependent on outside food aid.

"Frog in a well" was said about peasants who had not traveled outside their hamlets and had never seen Seoul. As

South Korea industrialized, the government cited the old expression to urge people to abandon inward-looking habits and search the world for export markets and new ideas.

So dwitgeoleume jwi japatda 소 뒷걸음에 쥐 잡았다

223 » The cow stepped on a rat while walking backward.

You got lucky, whether you deserved it or not.

Dak so bodeut, so dak bodeut 닭 소 보듯, 소 닭 보듯

224 » Like a hen looking at a cow; like a cow looking at a hen.

Looking at each other with utter indifference.

Sogeoleum 소걸음

225 » Cow-walking.

Foot-dragging. Stonewalling. "Cow-walking" was a fine art in the National Assembly, South Korea's one-house parliament. Legislators occasionally yelled, scuffled or blocked the entrances to the main legislative hall when a rival party tried to pass a bill they didn't like. They formed scrums, shoved their opponents or locked the speaker in his office to prevent him from convening a session. In several cases, the speaker let his deputy act on his behalf, and ruling party legislators gathered in the wee hours – catching their opponents off guard – and rammed through the bill so swiftly that all talk of cow-walking evaporated. Koreans called the tactic *nalchigi*, or "snatch and run."

Cheoncheonyi geoleodo hwangsogeoleum 천천히 걸어도 황소걸음

226 » The bull walks slowly, but it's still a bull's step.

Slowly but surely.

Mokmareun songyaji umul deulyeodabodeut 목마른 송아지 우물 들여다보듯

227 » You look like a thirsty calf looking into the well.

You want it but can't have it.

Jinagadeon gaega utgetda 지나가던 개가 웃겠다

228 » A passing dog would stop and burst out laughing.

That's preposterous.

Ttong muteun gae gyeo muteun gae namuranda 똥 묻은 개 겨 묻은 개 나무란다

229 » A dog smeared with excrement scowls at a dog smudged with chaff.

The pot calls the kettle black.

Gaebale ttamnanda 개발에 땀난다

230 » Even a dog's paws would sweat.

The situation was that hectic. Koreans believe dogs' paws are always dry.

Seodanggae samnyeone pungweol eupneunda 서당개 삼년에 풍월 읊는다

231 » After three years, even the school dog can recite a few poems.

If you hang around long enough, you'll learn something no matter how lazy or incompetent you are. The expression often ridicules someone who devotes a lot of effort to learning basic skills, but still can't perform.

A modern version: "After three years in Itaewon, a dog can sing a few American pop songs."

Seoul's Itaewon district is full of bars, restaurants and street markets catering to GIs from the nearby American 8th Army headquarters.

Dak jjotdeon gae kkol 닭 쫓던 개 꼴

232 » He resembles a dog chasing a chicken that has flown to the roof.

His efforts are in vain. "Stop waving your hands after the bus has left the station," people say to a man trying to win back his ex-girlfriend.

Gaereul jjoteul ttae domanggal gumungeul bogo jjotara 개를 쫓을 때 도망갈 구멍을 보고 쫓아라

233 » **When you chase off a dog, be sure it has an escape route.**

A cornered enemy will lash out in desperation.

Gaebale juseok pyeonja 개발에 주석 편자

234 » **Tin horseshoes on a dog's paws.**

An outlandish luxury. A total waste. Also: "A pearl necklace around a swine."

Gyeonwonjigan 견원지간

235 » **The relationship between a dog and monkey.**

A terrible relationship. The two animals don't get along.

Ji beoreut gae mot junda 지 버릇 개 못 준다

236 » **You can't throw your habit to a dog.**

It's hard to shed a bad habit.

Sanggatjip gae 상갓집 개

237 » **A dog in front of a house in mourning.**

An unwelcome guest. A ragged, emaciated person. When a

family organized a funeral, it was expected to put on a feast for visitors who came to pay tribute to the deceased. Inevitably, mongrels gathered around the house to scavenge for scraps. Barred from entering, they rarely cadged enough to ease their hunger.

Confucius spent much of his life wandering through China in search of a king who would recognize his philosophy as a wise tool of government. He was turned away repeatedly. Confucius compared himself in the wilderness days to a "dog in front of a house in mourning."

Daeboreumnal gae kkol 대보름날 개 꼴

238 》 I was like a dog during the first full moon festival.

In a sea of plenty, I had nothing. Poor families said this when they didn't have enough food for a big holiday festival.

Koreans used to greet the first full moon day of the Lunar New Year with a party. Food and liquor flowed, but celebrants never fed their dogs because they believed the dog and the moon were enemies. (According to Koreans, that's why you often find the dog growling at the moon). In Korean symbolism, the moon is female and the sun male. During the festival, it was said, the moon was at full strength, and village women were blessed by its power. But the dog could be a spoiler, barking and driving away the lunar magic. Thus villagers did not feed dogs so they would become weak and unable to challenge the moon.

239》 Dogs fighting in a mud pit. Yijeontugu 이전투구

Squabblers. This term originally described the people of Hamkyong, the northernmost province of what is now North Korea. They were known for tenacity and combativeness.

Chung Do-jon, a royal court minister, used this phrase when Yi Sung-ke, the founding king of the Yi Dynasty, asked him to describe the people of Hamkyong, the monarch's native province. When the king looked upset at the remark, the minister quickly added: "The Hamkyong people are also like bulls pulling plows in a rocky field." That pleased Yi.

Still, the Yi Dynasty cast a wary eye on Hamkyong and its adjacent Pyongan province. The government branded the regions as *banyeokhyeong*, or rebellious lands, because of frequent uprisings. The royal court discriminated against people from the regions in appointing government officials.

Today, life in the two northern provinces is harsher than elsewhere in communist North Korea. Many of the North Koreans who defect to the South come from the regions, which border with China and Russia.

240》 A dog never turns down excrement. Gaega ttongeul madaharya 개가 똥을 마다하랴

Koreans say this about officials who take bribes, hard drinkers who head for the bar after work, or children who can't stay out of the video game parlor.

In the old days, there was barely enough food for people, let alone dogs. So the animals scavenged. It was common to see dogs licking at human excrement. Koreans still refer to mongrels as "shit dogs."

Also: "A sparrow never passes a mill without stopping." It stops where the food is.

More dog expressions:

"You don't squabble with a dog over excrement." Don't argue with a scoundrel.

"A porridge bowl licked by a dog." A sarcastic reference to a man's spanking clean face.

"A stupid dog barks in the field." A put-down for a meddler. Dogs usually bark in the village.

"Even a dog recognizes its master." A snide comment for an ingrate.

Dwaeje myeokttaneun sori 돼지 멱따는 소리

241 》 He's squealing like a pig having its gullet cut.

I've never heard such a lousy singer. A useful barb in karaoke bars. But if a crooner makes you maudlin, say: "She is melting my liver and gallbladder." Or: "She finishes it off!" (*kkeutnae-junda!*) There's no competition. She's the best singer of the lot.

Seorimateun gureongyi gatyi 서리맞은 구렁이 같이

242 » She moved like a frostbitten serpent.

Groggy, lethargic.

Sajokeul danda 사족을 단다

243 » You're adding legs to a snake.

That's busywork. Stop beating around the bush! A snake slithers along just fine without legs. *Sajok*, or "snake's legs," means redundancy.

Eomuljeon kkolttugi 어물전 꼴뚜기

244 » The octopus in the fish stall.

A spoiler. *Kkolttugi* is a small octopus that spews out black ink, making it hard for fishmongers to keep their stalls spotless.

Yi japdeut dwijida 이 잡듯 뒤지다

245 » Search the area as if looking for lice.

Look into every nook and cranny. Leave no stone unturned. A South Korean TV news broadcast once said, "U.S. forces are scouring Afghan mountains for Osama bin Laden as if searching for lice."

Jjak ileun wonang 짝 잃은 원앙

246 » Mandarin duck that lost its spouse.

A lovelorn person. Mandarin ducks are a symbol of conjugal harmony. Newly married couples often keep a pair of wooden Mandarin ducks in their bedrooms. The ducks also adorn the embroidery of the pillows and blankets of a young couple. A wedding officiator urges the couple to "live like a pair of Mandarin ducks." Many wedding halls are named after the bird. Koreans believe a Mandarin duck that has lost its mate never finds another. Ornithologists say otherwise.

The wild goose symbolizes longevity; the crow, death; the magpie, good news. The white stork, with its long neck and white feathers, symbolizes grace and dignity; pine trees, incorruptibility; bamboo, righteousness.

Korean folding screens often show ten objects that symbolize long life: sun, cloud, mountain, rock, water, pine tree, stork, deer, turtle and mushroom.

Dakjang 닭장

247 » Chicken pen.

A discotheque. The term evokes the image of wild dancers, flapping like chickens in a coop. At the height of student protests in the 1980s, activists referred to a police bus as a "chicken pen." Framed by wire-screened windows, the disheveled detainees inside resembled caged birds.

248 » Country chicken.

Chondak 촌닭

An oaf, someone with crude manners who is unable to adapt to a new situation.

An old expression: "He looks like a country chicken under arrest at a government office."

249 » If not pheasant, then chicken.

Kkweong daesin dak 꿩 대신 닭

An imperfect alternative. Koreans customarily ate rice cake soup during the lunar New Year's Day, which usually falls in late January. Pheasant was an ideal ingredient in the soup, but it was hard to come by in winter. So many Koreans chose chicken, which had a similar taste.

250 » Pheasant chick.

Kkeobeongyi 꺼벙이

A klutz. A rustic. The term can also be affectionate, referring to a harmless bumbler. A pheasant, with its gleaming feathers, is one of the most colorful birds in Korea. But its chick has dark brown stripes, a drab look that camouflages it from predators in the underbrush.

Parents often choose the names of their children with the help of fortunetellers. But grandmothers sometimes bestow nasty nicknames such as “mongrel dog,” “dog dropping,” or “my ugly thing,” believing the monikers will make kids less vulnerable to disease or malicious spirits. It’s a form of camouflage, too.

At home, many girls used to be called *Kut-ja* or *Mal-ja*, which means “the last daughter.” The nickname reflected the parents’ hope that they would produce no more daughters; they wanted a boy.

After a few kidnapping cases made headlines in Korea in the 1990s, some mothers clad their children in tatty hand-me-downs rather than flashy designer clothes so kidnappers would not be tempted. A lesson from the pheasant.

Cheolsae 철새

251 » Migrant birds.

A derogatory term for politicians who change their affiliation for personal gain. If they’re not happy where they are, they bolt from their party and settle in a new political nest.

Kkamagiga hyeongnim hagetda 까마귀가 형님 하겠다

252 » A crow will call you a brother.

A mother says this to a grimy boy who returns home after playing outdoors all day long. Also: “A crocodile will call you a sister.” She’s got acne or rough skin.

Baepsaega hwangsae jjochagamyeon garangyi jjiteojinda 뱁새가 황새 쫓아가면 가랑이 찢어진다

253» If a titmouse tries to catch up with a stork, its crotch will split.

Don't overexert yourself. Set reasonable goals.

Ttwieobaya byeoruk 뛰어봐야 벼룩

254» Even if a tick can jump, it's still a tick.

Know your limits. Also, "You can't get away from Buddha's palm." An arrogant monkey that could ride clouds ridiculed Buddha for moving too slowly. Buddha said that even if the animal flew away from him as fast as possible for a month, it still could not get away. The monkey accepted the challenge and took off. After a month, it approached a huge mountain soaring up through clouds, blocking its way. It was Buddha's hand.

Mikkuraji han mariga onwumul heurinda 미꾸라지 한 마리가 온 우물 흐린다

255» One loach can muddy the whole well.

A rotten apple spoils the whole barrel. "Loach" is also slang for a slippery character, or a maverick in an organization full of conformists.

256 » A loach has become a dragon.

A rags-to-riches story. Often said with envy or derision. It can suggest that the person who has acquired a prize or high position does not deserve it. A variant: "He is a case of a dragon rising from a ditch" (*gecheoneseo yong natda*).

Koreans believed dragons controlled rain, fog, lightning and thunderclaps, and rode clouds. They represent power, authority and kings. The king's face was *yongan*, or "dragon face." The throne was *yongjwa*, or "dragon seat."

Deungyongmun, or "climb through the dragon gate," means to win a significant government post. The Dragon Gate was also upstream in the Yangtze River, where currents were so rapid that it was said the fish that swam up them became dragons.

Yongbieocheonga, or the "Song of Dragons Ascending to Rule the Heaven," is an epic poem. Published in 1447, it is the first literary work written in the Korean alphabet. It eulogizes the founding fathers of the Yi Dynasty. All Koreans know the poem's opening lines:

"A tree with a deep root is not shaken by the wind; it bears good flowers and many fruits.

"A deep well never dries up in drought; it flows, becomes a stream and reaches the sea."

257 » The dragon stream.

Mirinae 미리내

The Milky Way galaxy. Koreans believed dragons lived in seas and rivers. They ascended to heaven after their time on earth, and resided in the Milky Way. Some Korean streams are called *mirinae*. All such streams or rivers have stories about dragons. Koreans call a tornado *yongoreum*, or "a dragon rising to heaven."

258 » Dragon-whisker steel.

Yongsucheol 용수철

A spring, coil. In paintings, the Korean dragon looks like a large serpent with shiny scales, a wild hog's snout, deer antlers, four legs with eagle claws and fish fins on its back and tail. It has coiled whiskers. It breathes fire and carries a large red bead called *yeouiju*, or "magic bead," in its mouth or one of its claws. In folk tales, men seek the dragon bead, which had the power to make their dreams come true.

Dragons were of many colors. The roller coaster in an amusement park is a "blue dragon train" because it "flies" through the air.

Yongdusami 용두사미

259 » It has a dragon's head but a snake's tail.

A project that starts with a bang and ends with a whimper. Also, "He started drawing a tiger but ended up with a cat."

An entrepreneur who starts up his own business rather than working in a big corporation says: "I would rather be a snake's head than a dragon's tail."

Yongjaenghotu 용쟁호투

260 » Tiger and dragon fight.

A fierce duel.

Jaejuneun gomyi burigo doneun jungguksaramyi beonda 재주는 곰이 부리고 돈은 중국사람이 번다

261 » The bear does the stunts, but its Chinese owner collects the money.

One person sows and another reaps. This expression stems from Korean observations of Chinese circus troupes that traveled to Korea in the early 20th century. Koreans developed stereotypical views of Chinese as slow and stingy. An old Korean song makes fun of a penny-pinching Chinese silk trader named Mr. Wang who had a crush on a beautiful Korean kisaeng, or female dancer, and wasted all his money on her.

Gomege ae matginda 곰에게 애 맡긴다

262 » That's like asking a bear to baby-sit.

In a folk tale, a tame bear was baby-sitting. The bear was frazzled by flies that buzzed about the baby's face. Finally, it lifted a large stone and smashed it on the flies crawling on the baby's face.

Also, "That's like asking your cat to keep a fish for you."

Pari mal kkori japgo cheolee ganda 파리 말 꼬리 잡고 천리 간다

263 » A fly can travel a thousand miles on a horse's tail.

A horse could run a great distance without stopping. It always held its nose high, snorting and looking down on other creatures. One day, a fly sat on the horse's back.

"You dumb beast, stop being so highbrow. I can race a thousand miles as fast as you," the fly said.

The haughty horse threatened to stomp on the fly unless it proved its worth. The race began. The horse galloped and arrived fresh at the finish line. It looked back, thinking the fly was far behind.

"Now do you believe me?" said the fly, clinging to the horse's tail.

Today, the proverb ridicules the fly, rather than the horse. It describes someone of dubious worth who raises his own stature by sponging off those with real power.

Wonsungyido namuehseo tteoleojinda 원숭이도 나무에서 떨어진다

264 » Even a monkey falls from the tree.

Even a master makes mistakes.

Horangyi dambae piudeon sijeol iyagi 호랑이 담배 피우던 시절 이야기

265 » That's from an era when tigers smoked tobacco.

Something quaint, outdated. In old paintings, a tiger puffs tobacco through a long bamboo pipe. Once a luxury item, tobacco was fitting for the "king of the woods." A long pipe was a status symbol.

Some historians say Japanese invaders first brought tobacco to Korea in the late 1590s. It was widely used as medicine. People inhaled tobacco smoke to ease toothaches or bellyaches caused by parasites, and smeared tobacco-stained saliva on insect bites. One of the earliest reports on tobacco in Korea appears in *Jibongyuseol*, Korea's first encyclopedia, written by Lee Soo-kwang in 1614: "Sick people inhale the smoke through a bamboo pipe, and the smoke curls out of the nostrils. It reduces phlegm and repels a drunken stupor. Many people grow the plant for medical purposes. But the plant has poison and people should be warned against abusing it."

Tobacco was called "dambago" in old Korea. Lee's book says it was named after a southern Chinese woman who got rid of her chronic phlegm with tobacco. But linguists say "dambago" was more likely a distorted pronunciation of 'tobacco.'

Horangyi eopneun supe tokkiga wang noreuthanda 호랑이 없는 숲에 토끼가 왕 노릇한다

266 » When the tiger is absent from the woods, the rabbit acts like the king.

When the cat's away, the mice will play. In folk tales, the tiger is fierce and righteous. But it also puts on airs and falls into its own trap or is outwitted by a rabbit and other lesser creatures.

The tiger is said to fear dried persimmon the most.

Mothers and grandmothers delighted children with dried persimmon, a delicacy, on long winter nights. One evening, a ravenous tiger searched for a plump kid to swallow. Near a hut, he heard a bawling boy. Inside, the mother tried everything to stop the crying, pampering and threatening the kid. No luck. She finally said that if the boy kept crying, a tiger would come and eat him. To the eavesdropping tiger's chagrin, the kid cried even louder. Then the mother said one word and the kid stopped sniffling.

Gotgam, dried persimmon, was the word. Thinking it was a fierce animal, the tiger fled, tail between its legs.

Hareutgangyaji bum museowun jul moreunda 하룻강아지 범 무서운 줄 모른다

267 》 A one-year-old dog does not fear a tiger.

Fools rush in where angels fear to tread.

Bumdo ji malhamyeon onda 범도 지 말하면 온다

268 》 If you keep talking about the tiger, it will appear.

Talk of the devil. The tiger has a supporting role in Korea's foundation myth. Thousands of years ago, an illegitimate son of the Creator descended to Korea. He offered to turn a tiger and bear into man and woman if they ate only garlic and mugwort in a dark cave for 100 days. The restless tiger quit the test. But the bear, accustomed to hibernating, endured the ordeal and became a so-called "bear woman." The Creator's son didn't have a mate on hand for the woman, so he stood in himself. Their son grew up to become Tan-gun, the first leader of the Korean nation.

Note that the bear's stoicism prevailed over the tiger's impetuosity.

Jara bogo nolran gaseum sottukkeong bogo nolranda 자라 보고 놀란 가슴 솥뚜껑 보고 놀란다

269 》 A person who was once bitten by a tortoise gets startled when she sees a pot lid.

Once bitten, twice shy. Families used black cast-iron cooking pots with lids shaped like tortoise shells.

Goyangyi moke bangwul dalgi 고양이 목에 방울 달기

270 》 Tying a bell around a cat's neck.

An unpopular task. A cat lived in a rich man's house, which had an overflowing granary. The mice of the house could not grab any of the grain, fearing the cat would pounce on them. One night, a mouse had an idea.

"We should tie a bell around the cat so that we can hear the bell and know the cat is coming."

The mice were tickled by this triumph of ingenuity until one posed a tricky question.

"So who is going to tie the bell on the cat's neck?" Silence fell.

The mice are still debating the issue even tonight. You can hear them squeaking in the barn, their eyes twinkling.

Goraessaume saeu deung tteojinda 고래싸움에 새우 등 터진다

271 》 A shrimp gets its back broken in a whale fight.

The weak and helpless suffer when big powers collide. Office workers mutter this phrase when rival managers make their staff work longer hours. Koreans often describe their country's history in the last century with this expression.

After foreign powers forced Korea to open up to the outside world in the late 19th century, the nation became a pawn of regional powers, none of which wanted a rival to dominate a peninsula strategically located on major East Asian trade routes. Japan defeated China and Russia and ruled Korea from 1910 until the end of World War II, when the peninsula became a Cold War field of contest. On July 25, 1950, North Korea invaded the South in a bid to unify the nation under a communist banner. China and Russia aided the North, and American troops led U.N. forces on the South's side. The war dragged on for three years and ended with the battle lines drawn roughly where they started out.

Daramjwi chetbakwi dolgi 다람쥐 쳇바퀴 돌기

272 » The squirrel running on its wheel.

The tedious, repetitive life of city-dwellers. This expression is most often used by male, middle-aged office workers, and housewives. It's not as common among young people. Leisure activities such as overseas travel are far more widespread today than a generation ago.

Goyangyi jwi sanggakhagi 고양이 쥐 생각하기

273 » You're acting like a cat that says it feels sorry for a mouse.

You liar!

11 Family Matters

Men are top dogs in the Korean family,
and many phrases reflect that.
Women, though, are becoming more assertive.

274 » She is scratching the gourd.

Bagaji geulneunda 바가지 긁는다

Nag, nag, nag. In old Korea, women split a gourd, extracted the contents and used the empty shell as a dipper, an essential kitchen utensil. The grating, monotonous sound of scraping the bottoms of pots and water jars with the gourd dipper reminded husbands of the constant scolding of wives.

People made a similar noise with a gourd when a relative contracted cholera, believing it would exorcise the disease's spirit.

275 » He is stirring up wind.

Baram piunda 바람 피운다

He's having a fling. The expression derives from a cock or gander fluffing its feathers and beating its wings, stoking wind to attract a mate. Some housewives tell their husbands not to eat chicken wings lest they be tempted to "stir up wind." Most women joke about the superstition these days, but some leave out chicken wings when they fill their husbands' bowls.

Wind is fleeting, so an affair is not expected to last long.

Ttal set sijip bonaemyeon jip gidung muneojinda 딸 셋 시집 보내면 집 기둥 무너진다

276 》 After you have married off three daughters, the pillars of your house will fall down.

This is a common gripe about the financial strain of a dowry on a bride's family.

In earlier times, a costly wedding took place in the bride's house. The couple wore gowns of red, blue, green and yellow modeled on royal costumes. During the ceremony, the bride refrained from smiling. A smile supposedly doomed her to bear only girls, a dreadful prospect in a society where a wife was expected to perpetuate the male family line.

After the nuptial night, the couple traveled to the bridegroom's house. The husband rode a horse, trailed by his bride in a wooden sedan chair. A cortege of porters bore her dowry: household items, clothing, food, jade and gold trinkets for her husband's family. Her family's reputation was judged by the size of the dowry.

A variant: "If you have married off your three daughters, you can sleep with your doors open" (because there is nothing left for thieves).

"Getting married without a wooden sedan." This originally referred to a woman implicated in a scandal who married secretly, lest a public wedding draw unsavory comments from villagers. Today, it means: doing without formality in any context.

277 » ## A daughter as garnish.

Gomyeongttal 고명딸

A sole daughter in a household crowded with boys.

Ttal hana yeol adeul an bureopda 딸 하나 열 아들 안 부럽다

278 » ## One good daughter is worth ten sons.

This 1970s government slogan became a common expression. The state began the campaign because so many women only wanted sons and illegally aborted female fetuses. Authorities are still trying to end the trend. Doctors can lose their licenses for performing abortions or revealing the gender of fetuses through ultrasound tests. But when a pregnant mother asks if it's a boy, some doctors drop a hint. "You may have good news soon," they say. Or "Congratulations!" Or they smile.

Paleun aneuro gupneunda 팔은 안으로 굽는다

279 » ## Arms bend inward.

Charity begins at home. Koreans form strong bonds based on school, hometown or family ties. Many vote for candidates from their regions, regardless of merit.

"The crawfish sides with the crab," they also say. Birds of a feather flock together.

Koreans call it *kkiri kkiri*, or "together, together," disease.

Until 1997, four successive presidents came from South

and North Gyongsang Provinces in the southeast. Their critics accused them of encouraging regionalism to win votes and, once in office, appointing people from their home provinces to key government posts. Kim Dae-jung, a longtime foe of authoritarian governments who came from the rival southwestern Cholla region, was elected president in 1997. His opponents quickly accused him of similar favoritism.

Kim's predecessor, Kim Young-sam, was from South Gyongsang Province. On the campaign trail, one of his aides urged voters in neighboring North Gyongsang Province to vote for his boss.

Uriga namyiga! he declared. "We are not strangers!"

Koreans say this when they stress family connections. In a political context, the expression symbolizes the regional divisions that mark South Korean politics.

Kkamakwido gohyang kkamakwineun bangapda 까마귀도 고향 까마귀는 반갑다

280》 You will be happy to see even a crow if it comes from your hometown.

Hometown ties are that strong. The crow is a symbol of death.

Kkaega ssotajinda 깨가 쏟아진다

281》 Sesame seeds are pouring down.

Koreans say this about a couple with stars in their eyes. The blissful early days of newlyweds remind Koreans of a sesame harvest. In autumn, farmers cut sesame plants and dry them under the sun. They hang the stalks upside down and gently beat them with a stick. The sesame seeds cascade to the ground. The saying hints that good times pass quickly.

Manuraga yepeumyeon cheogatjip malttuk bogo jeolhanda 마누라가 예쁘면 처갓집 말뚝 보고 절한다

282 » If you love your wife, you bow to a dead tree in your in-laws' home.

You love everything about her.

Bujatjip matmyeonurigam 부잣집 맏며느리감

283 » She's fit to marry the first son of a rich family.

This used to be a high compliment for a woman. No longer. It means she is a sturdy homemaker, not afraid to roll up her sleeves at a family function, command an army of servants and, if necessary, clear away the dishes herself. Today, many young women strive to slim down and seek professional careers despite family pressure to get married right away and become full-time housewives.

A traditional Korean beauty had "a face like a bright full moon, brows like a crescent moon, lips like cherries, a waist like a willow branch, a soft, elegant walk, and a voice like a pearl rolling on a jade dish." These are stock phrases from old literature.

Some parents send their sons and daughters to special schools that try to help them gain height with jumping, stretching and other customized exercises. Retired basketball players run such facilities.

Sawineun baeknyeonjigaek 사위는 백년지객

284 » Your son-in-law is a guest who visits you once in 100 years.

Always treat your son-in-law as though you were never going to have another chance to host him. A mother fears an indifferent attitude toward a son-in-law will cause problems for her daughter. A young man is polite to his mother-in-law, who will most likely talk down to him. But she goes out of her way to feed him well. In the old days, a mother slaughtered the family's plumpest chicken when her son-in-law visited.

"Did your mother-in-law slaughter a chicken?" is a common expression today. It means: Did you have a feast when you visited your wife's family?

Konggaru jipan, kong pokkneun jipan 콩가루 집안, 콩 볶는 집안

285 » The family always roasts beans.

The family never stops bickering. Beans jump like popcorn when roasted in a pot. Pulverized with mortar and pestle, roasted beans are an ingredient in rice cake. "A bean powder family" is a family or organization full of strife.

Uneun ae jeot deo junda 우는 애 젖 더 준다

286》 You feed more milk to a crying baby.

Make a fuss and you'll get what you want. Today, most mothers feed powdered milk to their babies. Until a few decades ago, mothers breast-fed their children whenever they cried. When a mother had more than one baby, competition grew for her breast milk. A baby would take possession of both breasts, drinking milk from one and grasping the other to deny access to a sibling.

LIFE OF A CHILD

Until the 1970s, most babies were delivered at home. The midwife, usually an old, experienced villager, cut the umbilical cord with a pair of scissors. She tied its end with thread and cauterized it. The father burned the afterbirth with straws on the cleanest spot on his front yard.

After the birth, the family draped *geumjul*, or an "off-limits rope," across the gate of the house. Studded with pine branches or bamboo leaves, the rice straw rope barred outsiders from entering the house for three weeks. If the baby was a boy, the rope was also studded with red peppers, symbols of the male genitals. For a baby girl, lumps of charcoal were hung on the rope. According to superstition, a woman would bear a boy if she ate red peppers from the off-limits rope. Hence women avidly sought them. Koreans call both pepper and a baby boy's genitals *Gochu*.

A mother who lacked breast milk often chewed food and fed morsels to the baby. If a mother died or was short of milk, the baby's older sister carried it on her back to beg milk from nursing mothers in the neighborhood. To wean a child, mothers often smeared pepper powder or soot around their nipples to discourage the baby from seeking milk.

A mother toilet-trained a boy by placing him in front of a chamber pot, touching his genitals lightly and saying "sheeee..." to encourage urination. She also said "ung ga, ung ga..." to suggest defecation. It's common even today to hear a toddler saying "ung ga, ung ga." This babyspeak means: "Mom, change my diaper."

A child who lagged in toilet-training had to put a large sieve over his head, knock on neighbors' doors and ask to "borrow salt." Strict parents threatened not to let the embarrassed child in the house unless he returned with salt. They believed the humiliation would cure the child of a bed-wetting habit.

On its first birthday party, a baby is put in front of a low table stacked with food and fruits and formally introduced to relatives. The baby wears a special costume with golden stripes on the sleeves. It also wears a brimless silk hat with the Chinese characters for "good fortune" and "long life" embroidered on the sides. Relatives come with gifts of money or gold rings.

Uncles and aunts place a writing brush, money, bow and other objects on the birthday table and urge the baby to pick one. If the baby grabs a writing brush, a life of study lies ahead. Paper money signals success in business. The bow heralds a shining military career. Sometimes, a baby shows no interest or lunges for a slew of objects.

As a boy grew up, his grandfather fashioned a kite, a bow and arrow, or other toys. Boys whipped tops on frozen rice paddies in winter. Girls played hide-and-seek or *gonggi*, a marbles-like game with pebbles. Boys also made whistles from poplar bark. They played with *jegi*, a shuttle cock-like object made with a coin and mulberry paper. They kicked the object into the air with their instep and competed to see how many times they could kick it aloft without it dropping to the ground. The game is still popular.

Girls liked to jump straw ropes. When rubber became available, girls danced and sang over a black rubber rope held at each end by their friends. The girl dancing on the rope had to make a prearranged set of turns and jumps. She "died" if she made a mistake, then held the rubber rope for another girl. The boys were a menace. They hid behind a wall and rushed out, cutting the rope with a penknife and running away. Some girls chased the boys, wielding sticks and throwing stones.

jasik nongsaboda deo
Jungyohan nongsa eopda 자식 농사보다 더 중요한 농사 없다

287 》 There is no harvest more important than a harvest of children.

Koreans say a family with polite kids who do well at school and beyond has "a good harvest of children." South Korea was predominantly agricultural until it began industrializing in the 1970s. Hence the harvest analogy.

More expressions on the traditional family:

- "If you love your grandson, you eat his snivel-smeared rice."
- "A spoiled child pulls at the grandfather's beard." Be stern with children because bad habits are hard to correct.
- "There is no son like his father; there is no brother like his older brother." The hierarchy of family.
- "A woman and dried pollack: the more you beat them, the better they taste." Or "a man must beat his wife once every three days to make her behave." These expressions are no longer popular.

Yeol songarak muleoseo an apeun
songarak eopda 열 손가락 물어서 안 아픈 손가락 없다

288 》 If you bite your ten fingers, every single one hurts.

Every child is dear to you.

Goseumdochido ji jasikeun yeppeuda 고슴도치도 지 자식은 예쁘다

289 » The hedgehog is beautiful in the eyes of its mother.

No mother thinks she has a bad-looking kid. People also say, "Even if she were to drop her baby in her eye, it wouldn't hurt."

Ae apeseoneun chanmuldo mot masinda 애 앞에서는 찬물도 못 마신다

290 » When children are around, you can't even drink water.

Watch your words and deeds when children are present. If children see you drink water, they are likely to ask for water as well.

An old Buddhist monk kept persimmons in his temple room and did not give any to a young apprentice, telling the boy that the fruits would poison children.

One day, when the old monk was away, the boy ate all the persimmons, broke a jar of honey and climbed a tree to wait for his teacher to return. The monk went berserk when he saw what had happened. Perched safely in the tree, the boy said: "Dear Master, I shattered your honey jar by mistake. It was such a grave sin that I thought I should kill myself. So I ate all your poisonous fruits, but how strange! I am still alive."

The old monk laughed and forgave the boy.

Tteokdukkeobi gateun adeul nara 떡두꺼비 같은 아들 낳아라

291 》 I wish you would give birth to a boy that looks like a fat toad.

A pregnant woman wants to hear this wish. To many Koreans, a toad symbolizes a plump, healthy baby boy. Parents used to feed roasted frog legs to sickly children.

Gaji maneun namue baram jalnal eopda 가지 많은 나무에 바람 잘 날 없다

292 》 A tree with many branches is always shaken by the wind.

A mother with a large brood doesn't get a moment of peace. When a child falls sick or gets into trouble, parents sigh and say: "The best luck is childless luck."

A mother with many toddlers compares her endless chores to "putting shoes on a centipede."

Contraceptives were once scarce and couples produced as many children as they could. Under Confucian mores, people regarded the failure to produce children as a grave offense to their ancestors. The birth of twins and triplets was seen as an omen of good harvest.

Old villages teemed with children. Their mortality rate was so high until the 1940s that many parents took out birth certificates only after their children overcame measles and other diseases, and reached one or two years of age. Many old Koreans have two ages: one registered in government records, and their real age. When a Korean says he is 76 years old, chances are that he is actually two or three years older.

When epidemics struck a village, many parents did not bury dead children because interment of such bodies was believed to bring more death. Instead, they wrapped the corpses in white cloth and placed them on pine tree branches. In a year of epidemics, the valley was marked by white dots. Magpies, crows and other carrion birds fed on the bodies. Eventually, the remains fell to the ground. Even when families buried their dead children, the graves lacked the usual mounds and headstones because of the Confucian belief that it was a sin for children to die before their parents.

The most feared disease was smallpox. Helpless parents held the epidemic in awe, calling it *sonnim* ("respected guest") or *mama* ('Your Highness' in the royal court).

"I hope you get typhoid" is a common insult today.

Hakeultteda – or "I finally got rid of the malaria" – means: I'm finally free of a nagging problem, or a harrowing experience is over at last. This expression is popular today, though malaria expressions like these are fading:

"The bus is rattling as if it had malaria."

"It was so cold that I shook like a dog with malaria."

Bubussaumeun kalro mul begi 부부싸움은 칼로 물 베기

293 » A quarrel between man and wife is like slashing water in half with a knife.

A couple's argument never lasts.

Jipeseo saeneun bagaji pakeseodo saenda 집에서 새는 바가지 밖에서도 샌다

294 » The gourd dipper that leaks at home leaks outside as well.

A good family member is a good citizen. The phrase stresses the importance of a stern upbringing at home.

Nopasim 노파심

295 » An old woman's mind.

An elderly woman's mind crowds with worries about her children away from home. Today, *nopasim* means unnecessary worries. When Koreans voice concern or advise caution, they often say, "It may sound like *nopasim*, but...."

Byeonghwan samnyeone hyoja eopda 병환 삼년에 효자 없다

296 » After three years of looking after an ill parent, no son will be faithful any more.

Loyalty dissolves after prolonged hardship. Most parents live with their eldest sons. Despite Confucian emphasis on filial devotion, the burden of caring for sick parents could wear out a son's loyalty.

The proverb highlights that hardship, and is not meant to be taken literally. Korea is rich with fictional stories about children who did extraordinary things for their sick parents. A daughter, Shim Chong, sold herself for 300 bushels of rice to help her blind father. Fishermen threw her into the Yellow Sea as a human sacrifice to quell a stormy sea. The Dragon God saved her. After returning to land, she married the king and her blind father was so delighted by his daughter's miraculous return that he recovered his sight. During a famine, a son cut flesh from his thigh and cooked it to feed his sick parent. He pretended it was beef.

In the ancient Koryo Kingdom, some peasants abandoned their old parents in the hills because they were a drain on family resources. Historians differ on whether this practice, called "Koryo funeral," was widespread.

Jaldoemyeon nae tat, motdoemyeon josang tat 잘되면 내 탓, 못되면 조상 탓

297》 When things go well, he praises himself. When things go badly, he blames his ancestors.

He never takes the blame. Koreans believed much of their fortune depended on the blessing of dead ancestors.

It was common to hear people say, "I thank my ancestors!" when they won an award. In tough times, they lamented, "Dear ancestors, how come you are so indifferent toward me."

The Confucian tradition of ancestral worship dominates family rituals. Koreans believe they and their children will have good luck if they worship their ancestors diligently. This helps explain why millions head to their hometowns during major holidays, despite grueling traffic jams. Seoul, a city of 10 million people, seems almost deserted during the lunar New Year's and Chusok full-moon autumn harvest holidays. People in traditional dress climb hills to pay tribute to ancestral graves with rice cake, rice wine, dried fish and fruits. They perform similar rituals during the anniversaries of their ancestors' deaths.

DEATH

Until the early 20th century, some sons built huts beside the graves of deceased parents and stayed there for three years, mourning and tending the grave. They were not allowed to marry during this time.

When a parent died, a rich family hired a geomancer to search for a propitious grave site. The size of the funeral rite depended on the wealth and status of the bereaved family. In a traditional funeral procession, dozens of men – the number depended on the family's wealth – bore large silk or hemp banners streaming from bamboo poles with bells at their tips. The banners bore eulogies to the deceased. Porters wearing cloth harnesses carried a bier on a heavy pinewood framework the size of a modern bus. The family decorated the bier with red, yellow and white paper or silk. A man led the procession, ringing a bell and singing funeral songs in cadences that helped the slow-moving funeral bearers keep in step and frightened away evil spirits from the path of the deceased.

Heads bowed, male family members walked with sticks in their hands, stooping and wailing. The women of the family held long bands of white cloth tied to the bier. The bands symbolized the link between the deceased and the offspring.

All funeral participants wore clothes of white, the traditional funeral color. Some women collapsed and blocked the procession in a respectful show of reluctance to part with the deceased _ until friends came along to help them off the route. Rich families hired professional wailers.

The bier was burned at the grave site to provide the deceased with transportation to the afterworld. The Yi Dynasty kings and governments of modern Korea tried to curtail the long mourning period and extravagant ceremonies related to death.

Today, hospitals have funeral houses where the family builds a shrine lined with chrysanthemums, and relatives and friends come to pay tribute with cash envelopes. The family plies guests with food and liquor. It was considered a good custom for guests to stay overnight, drinking and playing card games. For many men, going to funerals used to be a good excuse to come to work late the next morning. The government banned the practice in hospitals in the 1990s to cut waste.

After North Korean leader and founder Kim Il Sung died in 1994, his son and successor, Kim Jong Il, observed a three-year mourning period. The junior Kim refrained from making public appearances, adding to the mystery of the country and speculation that his authority was wobbly. The younger Kim's show of filial piety fused his persona with that of his father and solidified the personality cult he inherited.

Confucianists revered the body, a gift from ancestors. So cremation was not widespread, nor is it popular today. Public cemeteries are overcrowded.

12
Luck, Dreams, Superstitions

Korea has been around for 5,000 years.
Some of its superstitions are shamanistic.
Some are based on Confucian beliefs.
Others are plain weird.

Wen tteokyinya? 웬 떡이냐?

298 » Where did this rice cake come from?

A windfall.

Hobakyi neongkulchae gulreo deuleowatda 호박이 넝쿨 채 굴러 들어왔다

299 » A pumpkin rolled into my home with its vine and all.

I got lucky. Pumpkins abound in rural Korea. Their vines spread over roofs and mud-and-stone walls and frontyard persimmon trees. Sometimes a neighbor's pumpkin falls from a branch and rolls into the garden next-door.

Pumpkins and gourds often appear in Korean folk tales as conduits for good luck or misfortune. A bird, for example, brings a good man a seed that grows into a gourd stuffed with gold coins. A bad man's gourd spews excrement or snakes.

Daebak teojyeotda 대박 터졌다

300 » A big gourd exploded.

It was a hit. Say this about a lottery winner, a bestselling book or a movie blockbuster.

Bagaji deopeosseotda 바가지 덮어썼다

301 » I had a gourd dipper on my head.

I got ripped off. Or I was humiliated. You look foolish with a hollowed-out gourd on your head.

Ttong bagaji, or "shit dipper," had a long handle and was widely used by farmers to scoop up waste from the outhouse pit and spread it in the fields as fertilizer.

"I had a shit scoop on my head." I was humiliated. All the blame fell on me.

Farmers often converted plastic military helmet liners into excrement dippers. Thus a "shit dipper" was a derogatory nickname for a military policeman who wore a shining helmet liner.

Jaesu om buteotda 재수 옴 붙었다

302 » My luck has scabies.

I'm jinxed.

Jaesu eopseumyeon dwiro jappajyeodo koga kkaejinda 재수 없으면 뒤로 자빠져도 코가 깨진다

303 » When you're unlucky, you get a nosebleed even when you fall on your back.

Sometimes, nothing goes right. Also: "If you're unlucky, you can drown in a dish."

Guk sotgo heobeokji dego 국 쏟고 허벅지 데고

304 » He spilled his hot soup and burned his thigh.

From bad to worse.

Dorumuk 도루묵

305 » Return to muk.

Return to obscurity after fleeting fame. Sun Jo, a 16th century king, was fleeing Seoul as Japanese plunderers approached. A fisherman gave a silver fish to the starving king, who thought it was so delicious that he asked its name. The fisherman said the fish was "muk," which means silent and worthless in Korean. Sun Jo ordered his government to rename it "Silver Fish."

After the Japanese invaders retreated, the king returned to Seoul and wanted to eat the fish again. By now, Sun Jo had been spoiled by succulent palace food, and he found the fish tasteless. He scowled and said, "Give the fish its old name back."

A project that bombs after showing initial promise "returns to muk."

Ganeunnalyi jangnal 가는 날이 장날

306 » It was a market day when I went to town.

You never know your luck. Itinerant markets opened every five days, as they still do in the countryside today. When a farmer went to town on a separate errand and found the market open as well, he was probably happy to get two chores done in the same day.

Market day was one of the few sources of entertainment in those days because circus clowns, snake-oil sellers and whatnot showed up along with regular traders.

The phrase often refers to an unfortunate coincidence. Someone who travels a long way to a shop but finds an item sold out will grumble: "What bad luck! It was a market day when I went to town."

Baram matahtda 바람맞았다

307 » I only met the wind.

She stood me up. A person "hit by the wind" has suffered a stroke. People call the ailment "the wind" because it strikes with few visible symptoms.

Jwigumeongedo byeotdeulnal itda 쥐구멍에도 볕들 날 있다

308 » Even the rat hole sometimes gets the sun.

Every dog has its day.

Doero jugo malro batneunda 되로 주고 말로 받는다

309 》 He gave a peck and got a bushel.

Sow the wind and reap the whirlwind.

Hok tteryeoda hok butyeotda 혹 떼려다 혹 붙였다

310 》 I tried to get rid of a cyst, but ended up with a second cyst.

A clumsy attempt to resolve a problem only made matters worse.

Dwaejikkum kkweotna? 돼지 꿈 꿨나?

311 》 Did you have a pig dream last night?

You're so lucky. When Koreans see, embrace or roll with a pig in their dreams, they buy a lottery ticket. A pig dream means luck, but don't talk about it because any listener will inherit its good fortune. If you have to tell someone, do so at night when it's harder for others to eavesdrop. As an extra precaution, call your dog's name three times to scare off any snoopers.

Koreans believe it's good luck to have dreams about eating raw meat, a cow walking into their house or a burning house. Woe betide those who dream of using a rake or plow, or being swept away in water. If you lose a tooth in your dreams, a relative may die. Laugh during a dream, and you may cry in the daytime.

"Dog dreams" are bad or meaningless.

Kkumboda haemongyi jotda 꿈보다 해몽이 좋다

312 》 Her interpretation was better than her dream.

She made a mountain out of a mole hill. People believe the dream of a pregnant woman – called a "dream of the womb" – foretells the baby's gender and future. An expectant mother who has a dream often consults fortunetellers, whose interpretations often vary widely. A mother may do her own interpretation and attach too much significance to the dream.

When a man becomes a Cabinet minister or president, rumors spread that his mother dreamed of a dragon when she was pregnant with the future luminary.

Eoseolpeun mudang saram japneunda 어설픈 무당 사람 잡는다

313 》 A clumsy sorcerer kills people.

Trouble awaits if you're not prepared. The "mudang," a female shaman or high priestess of ancient spirit worship, is still a presence in rural villages. The sorcerer performs dances to cure ailments and exorcise the demons that cause them.

MUDANG

Some rural folks still believe in spirits of the kitchen, household, great rocks, old trees and the dead. Old Koreans even worshipped spirits residing in the muck of the rice paddies and the fetid pit of the outhouse.

Each village had at least one shaman, whose tiled-roof temple stood out among the low-lying, farmers' huts. Her inspirations were sometimes eclectic: she might decorate her shrine with Buddhist paintings, worship a dead Confucian scholar and place rice and fruits before an old, crooked tree in an animistic ritual. Her temple was a place for communion with the spirits and the dead. The mudang told fortunes, interpreted dreams and helped villagers contact relatives in the afterworld. She was paid in cash, grain or cloth.

If herbal medicine failed, people resorted to the mudang to deal with disease-spreading spirits. Flanked by an aide playing a brass gong, she performed a lengthy exorcism dance called the 'gut' (pronounced 'good.')

Sorcery was widespread but its practitioners were near the bottom of the social class system, and were frowned upon by the Confucian elite of the Yi Dynasty. There were also male shamans called 'pansu,' but they were few and almost always operated alongside the mudang.

South Korea closed down many mudang shrines and discouraged their rituals during state-sponsored modernization in the 1970s, but the tradition lives on in rural pockets. Today, you can spot a mudang's house in villages because she keeps a long bamboo pole, a prop in her rituals, in her front yard. These days, few people resort to the mudang for serious medical treatment.

In the old days, families summoned their favorite mudang, *dangol*. Today, restaurants and pubs call their patrons *dangol*. At the peak of a performance, the mudang spoke the "language of the spirit," relaying the word of the deceased to her client. The process was called *neokduri*. The mudang also gave the villager a long tongue-lashing, or *punyeom*, on behalf of the spirit. Today, *neokduri* and *punyeom* both mean ravings or mumbled complaints.

Kkachiga ulmyeon joeun sosik itda 까치가 울면 좋은 소식 있다

314》 If a magpie cries near your house in the morning, it brings good news.

A king went mad and killed family members. He sent an old relative into exile on wind-swept Jeju, the southernmost island of Korea.

A decade later, a magpie perched on a tree outside her house and chattered three times (Three is a lucky number in Korea). Later that day, a courier from the royal court rushed in with good news: the mad king had been dethroned by a relative, who asked the old lady to return to the palace in Seoul. On her return sea voyage, she saw the same magpie on the ship's mast. The captain said he had earlier given the bird a ride from the mainland. But when the island came into sight, the bird took off and flew to the island ahead of the ship to deliver the good news before the royal messenger.

Koreans believe they can expect guests or good news if they see a magpie near their house in the morning.

The bird is the mascot of the Korean postal service.

Bap meokeul ttaeneun gaedo an ttaerinda 밥 먹을 때는 개도 안 때린다

315 » You don't even hit a dog when it's eating.

It's a taboo to scold somebody who is eating. Koreans traditionally frowned upon talking too much over food. In conservative families, the father usually does not say a word throughout the meal.

Taboos and superstitions in Korea are rooted in universal morality, Confucian edicts or shamanistic beliefs.

Many reflect prejudice against women. These expressions are losing punch, but they remain common in daily male chat, whether said in jest or earnestness.

- "If a woman talks too much, she will become a widow."
- "A woman who whistles will have bad luck."

Koreans don't whistle much. Mothers warn children that if

they whistle at night, a snake will enter their room.

● "If you have a female guest on the first day of the year, you will have bad luck all year. If your first customer of the day is a woman, your shop will do badly for the rest of the day."

Other taboos and superstitions:

● "Bad things happen if you greet people while barefoot."

Dress properly when greeting visitors.

● "You'll get the hiccups if you eat something you pilfered."

If somebody hiccups, Koreans often joke: "Did you eat something you stole?"

● "Step on dog droppings, and you will get lucky."

● "Steal shoes, and you'll become a snake in your next life."

Snakes don't wear shoes.

● "On a day of ancestral worship, untie the clothes line and keep your gate open for the spirits of dead ancestors."

The clothes line might trip the spirits. Koreans light a lantern on the evening of the ancestral rite so spirits can find the house. In some families, the patriarch flings open the door of the room where the rite is taking place. He bows and mumbles: "Dear ancestors, please come in and accept our offering." After many deep bows, the family leaves the room, shuts the door and waits quietly outside so the dead can feast in private. The food in ancestral rites is sacred. After the ritual, the family mixes it in a large bowl and eats it. That is the origin of *bibimbap*, a Korean dish of rice mixed with vegetables and whatever else is available.

Bibimbap was once for commoners who had to eat quickly and couldn't afford a full table of side dishes. Now, everybody eats it.

- "When your dog gives birth, don't wear colorful clothes."

The garments might distract the exhausted mother dog.

- "Don't sleep with your head pointing north."

The dead travel north.

- "If you scatter your nail clippings, bad things happen."

In a folk tale, a man always scattered his nail clippings. A rat ate all of them, turned itself into a replica of the man and kicked him out of his house. A Buddhist monk gave the man a cat, which slashed and killed the replica.

Weather superstitions:

- "Ants crossing the road in a long file herald rain."
- "If it snows a lot in winter, you will have a good harvest."
- "There's an end to drought, but there is no end to a flood."

Korean farmers feared floods more than drought. They often said: "A flood is like an old wife's nagging."

- "If a toad jumps into your house, it's going to pour."
- "When a tortoise crawls out of water and looks to the south, the weather will be fine. If it looks to the north, it will rain."

316 》 An inexperienced 'pungsu' ruins a family.

One clumsy worker can ruin an entire project. Pungsu, which means "wind and water," is a Korean geomancer. Koreans often seek advice from geomancers on where to build a new house or family graves. Kings sought their advice when they moved their capitals.

A good grave site is said to assure good fortune for the family, and a bad site scourges the family for generations. Water oozing from an ancestor's grave signals a looming family catastrophe.

GEOMANCY AND KOREAN HISTORY

Geomancers study topography and 'gi,' energy of the landscape, to select propitious burial sites.

Families might consider relocating the remains of ancestors if they find better sites. President Kim Dae-jung relocated the graves of his parents before the 1997 presidential election. Kim, a Roman Catholic, did not say whether he followed a geomancer's advice. But he won the vote and became president in his fifth attempt. The family of former Prime Minister Kim Jong-pil moved his father's remains in 2000. Newspapers wondered whether the move was politically motivated.

Tae Won Kun was a king's relative who was jobless but ambitious. A geomancer told him that his family would produce two kings in a row if he shifted his father's remains to a site in central South Korea. He followed the advice, burning down a Buddhist temple and removing its stone pagoda to make space for his father's remains in 1844.

Seven years later, his second son was born. At age 12, that son succeeded a childless relative to become King Ko Jong of the Yi Dynasty.

Tae Won Kun acted as regent for his son for a decade.

During his rule, Western ships turned up on Korea's shores. He regarded contact with Westerners and their ideas as dangerous. An incident involving his father's tomb led him to tighten his so-called *swaeguk* – or "closing the country with a chain lock" – policy of extreme seclusion.

A German adventurer, Ernest Oppert, twice asked permission to trade with Korea, but was rejected. He came ashore in 1868 to loot the tomb of Tae Won Kun's father at the new grave site. He plotted to force a trade deal in exchange for the remains and relics. Oppert's crew repelled tomb guards and burrowed into the enormous crypt, but retreated before reaching the coffin because the Yellow Sea tide was ebbing and armed villagers were mobilizing. Oppert's failed foray shocked Korea and Tae Won Kun grew more suspicious of foreigners. (The regard for a dead ancestor was so great that stolen corpses drew huge ransoms in old Korea, and wealthy families hired "tomb guards." In 1999, tomb-raiders dug up and demanded a ransom for the skeletal remains of the father of Shin Kyuk-ho, chairman of South Korea's lucrative Lotte business group. Police arrested two suspects and reclaimed the remains).

Western powers tried to open Korea with military force, resulting in two *yangyo*, or "foreign disturbances."

In 1866, Tae Won Kun executed nine French Catholic missionaries and thousands of Korean converts. The French Asiatic Squadron in China sent a flotilla of seven warships to retaliate. The forces landed on Kanghwa Island at the mouth of the Han River that led to Seoul, and fought fierce battles. The French detachment pillaged government archives on the island. Today, South Korea demands that France return the documents in a long-running diplomatic dispute.

In the same year, the General Sherman, an armed American ship carrying a Chinese crew and a few Americans, defied warnings and steamed up the Taedong River to the ancient Korean capital of Pyongyang to demand a trade deal. The ship exchanged fire with locals on shore. After a few days, the ship grounded in shallows and Koreans burned it, killing all 19 on board.

Five years later, five American warships landed marines on Kanghwa Island to avenge the General Sherman. American marines killed hundreds of Korean defenders. Local militia fought back with cannons in the first battle that Americans fought in Korea.

After these two episodes, Tae Won Kun erected stone

monuments on the Chongno thoroughfare in central Seoul and throughout the country. Their inscriptions read: "Western barbarians invade our land. If we do not fight, we must then appease them. To appease them is to sell off our nation. Ten thousand generations of Koreans must always bear this statement in mind."

Tae Won Kun's grandson was the dynasty's last king before Japan annexed Korea in 1910.

317» Eight letters. Palja 팔자

Palja is composed of two letters each for the year, month, date and hour a person was born. Fortunetellers "read the eight letters," interpreting their combination to tell a future. Many Koreans believe the eight letters determine their fate.

Frustrated people sigh in resignation and say, "That's my *palja*." When things get tough, some say: "The best *palja* is the dog's *palja*." They envy dogs, which lounge in the sun and don't worry about anything.

But, "You can't throw your *palja* to a dog."

"She changed her eight letters" means she changed her life. It usually means she remarried. "He corrected his eight letters" means he struck rich.

“Even Dong Bang Sak didn’t know his *palja*” means you never know when you will die. Dong Bang Sak was an eccentric official at an ancient Chinese court. Legend says he lived 180,000 years after eating peaches that he stole from a Himalayan goddess who governed immortality.

Another story says that Dong Bang Sak was originally destined to live only 1,800 years, but he wined and dined the envoy from the netherworld who came to collect him.

The corrupt envoy took the man to the underworld. While the king of darkness was asleep, he forged the books by adding two zeros to Dong Bang Sak’s life span. The next day, the king ordered Dong Bak Sak to head back up, saying there had been an accounting error.

After 180,000 years, Dong Bang Sak dodged the envoy who returned to escort him back down.

To catch Dong Bang Sak, the envoy disguised himself as a farmer and washed charcoal in a stream. After several days, reports of this strange activity spread. Dong Bang Sak showed up and asked what the man was doing.

“I am washing charcoal to make it white,” the envoy said.

“Are you crazy?” Dong Bang Sak snorted. “In my 180,000-year life, I’ve never heard of such a thing.”

Thus the envoy caught Dong Bang Sak. Curiosity killed the cat. In old Korea, people placed a small Dong Bang Sak doll in funeral biers to guide the deceased to the netherworld.

318 » A day without guests.

Son eopneun nal 손 없는 날

Families move to new houses on propitious days called "days without guests." The "guests" in this case are evil spirits. The lucky days usually fall on the ninth and tenth days of each month in the Asian lunar calendar. On these days, moving companies make a killing. In Seoul, families move in or out of high-rise apartment blocks, and it's easy to spot cranes hoisting furniture from or to balcony windows.

Many people consult fortunetellers about what dates they should marry off children and make investments. Someone who buys a car or opens a restaurant is likely to place a table of food and fruits in a ritual to prevent accidents and ensure prosperity.

Most fortunetellers operate in back-alley shops or street-corner tents. Some cast rice grains or sticks on a table. Others read lines on your face or palms. They draw symbols to ward off evil spirits. The art of predicting the future has gone online in South Korea. Net-surfers pay a fee for one-on-one sessions with "cyber fortunetellers."

Young Koreans consult fortunetellers over coffee at "saju (fortunetelling) cafes" near college campuses and on trendy streets in Seoul. The soothsayers are often college graduates who claim to have studied the Book of Changes, a Chinese classic on divination, or have an ability to consult a deity. Their biggest clients are young couples who want divine forces and the Zodiac to bless their relationships.

13
Borrowed From Buddhism

Many expressions with Buddhist roots assumed secular meanings. They talk about people who communicate without uttering a word or crave food as much as a starving monster.

319» Lion's roar.

Sajahu 사자후

The final word. When the lion roars, the animals in the bush tremble and fall silent. If you make a convincing argument, you "roar like a lion."

"Lion's roar" originally referred to Buddha's sermons, which set down the ultimate truth, quashing all other arguments, questions, opinions and speculation.

Buddhist sermons are full of rich, mystical metaphors and episodes.

320» Geondal.

Geondal 건달

Libertine. Hoodlum. Geondal is a Buddhist deity and patron of music. He inhales incense and floats around like fragrant smoke. The term was once used for musicians, who were considered lazy and low-class. Over the centuries, it became associated with the jobless, idlers and extortionists.

Koreans also call a thug *eokkae*, or "shoulder," because the stereotype has a thick chest. When Koreans see a brute, they say, "Who's that shoulder?" A thug is also *jumeok*, or "fist."

So gwie gyeong ilgi 소 귀에 경 읽기

321 » It's like reading Buddhist Sutras into the cow's ear.

Talking to a wall. Or "it's like a spring wind passing by the horse's ear" (*mayidongpung*). As meaningless to him as spring wind is to a horse.

Yadanbeopseok 야단법석

322 » Outdoor Buddhist sermon.

A commotion. In times of old, a Buddhist temple hosted an outdoor sermon and invited a large crowd. There were colorful decorations, music, and incense burning. It was boisterous. Today, temples host the same sermons but they are mostly held indoors and are subdued in comparison to rock festivals and other modern scenes.

Dolmaengyido meorireul kkeudeokhanda 돌맹이도 머리를 끄덕한다

323 » He is so persuasive that even stones (or stone Buddha statues) will nod their heads.

A Buddhist monk studied the art of preaching. During his grueling exercise, he placed a pile of stones in front of him and vowed to keep preaching until he converted the rocks to Buddhism. He knew he had made it when the stones began nodding to his sermons.

324 » Brass bell.

Dongnyang 동냥

The act of begging food, or food that has been begged. The term is a distortion of *dong-ryong*, a brass bell that monks carried when they begged from village to village. Today's monks prefer a wooden gong, though most no longer ask for food, partly because people frown upon beggars. Monks cook their own meals with donations from worshippers.

"You will live your life begging for food" (*bileomeokeul nom*) is a common curse.

Jeolyi sileumyeon, jungyi tteonanda 절이 싫으면, 중이 떠난다

325 » If a Buddhist monk doesn't like the temple, he leaves.

If you're not happy where you are, don't hang around. Go elsewhere.

Buddhist monks abandon temples when routine and comforts fray their devotion to the pursuit of enlightenment. Some stick around.

326 » From mind to mind.

Yisimjeonsim 이심전심

When two people know each other very well, they say, *Yisim jeonsim*. It means: "You don't have to say it; I know what you mean." It also means perfect teamwork.

Once Buddha picked a lotus flower and looked around at his students, without saying a word. The disciples thought hard to figure out what Buddha was trying to communicate, but Buddha gave no hint. After a while, one old student smiled. Out of that episode comes the phrase *yeomhwamiso*, or "Buddha picked up a flower and his student smiled." It means the same as *yisimjeonsim*.

When President Kim Young-sam didn't reveal his favorite among those competing for his party's presidential nomination in 1997, newspaper commentators wondered, "Who has won the Kim *sim* (mind)?"

In Buddhism, language is like a finger pointed at the moon, monks say. One must look beyond the finger, the language, to see the moon, but most people live their lives just looking at the finger, they say.

Koreans like to say, "She was wrong even before she opened her mouth."

WON HYO

Won Hyo, a Buddhist monk of the Shilla Kingdom, was on his way to China to seek enlightenment. One stormy night, Won

Hyo and his friend lost their way and stumbled into a cave. It was pitch-dark inside.

Overnight, Won Hyo's throat burned with thirst. Fumbling about, he found what felt like a bowl containing water. The water tasted sweet and Won Hyo went back to sleep. In the morning, Won Hyo vomited for hours. What he had drunk overnight was rain water in a blackened human skull, squirming with worms. When he regained his composure, an insight struck.

"The entire world is a fiction. It's only my mind that matters," Won Hyo told his friend. "The water in the skull was the same last night and this morning. But my mind conceived of it as sweet last night and revolting this morning. I'm going home. Enlightenment is already in my mind, and I don't need to go to China to find it."

Won Hyo became Korea's most famed – and eccentric – Buddhist monk. He rode a cow. He flouted the Buddhist taboos: he consumed alcohol and meat, teased women with obscene jokes and fathered a son named Sul-chong, who grew up to become a great scholar.

One day, the king heard that Won Hyo was wandering around, singing these cryptic lyrics: "I am going to carve a pillar that will shore up heaven. So who's going to lend me an axe without a handle?"

The king understood the metaphor: an axe without a handle was a woman's genitalia. The king ordered a widowed young princess to sleep with the monk.

327 ›› Temple son.

Jeoljip adeul 절집 아들

Bastard. It was considered a couple's paramount duty to produce a son to continue the family line. If the wife turned out to be barren, the family sometimes discreetly hired a surrogate mother. Some rich men also had concubines who bore them children. When a man appeared to be sterile, some families dispatched the wife to a Buddhist temple to pray for a son for 100 days.

In rare cases, the woman returned and gave birth. Since it was difficult to tell whether the husband was really sterile, the family adopted the child as its own. But rumor seeped out that the woman "brought the child from the temple." In other words, the child's real father was probably a monk.

328 ›› The Buddhist monk can't shave his own head.

Jungyi jye meori mot kkakneunda 중이 제 머리 못 깎는다

You can't do everything yourself. In Buddhism, "shaving the head" is a symbolic step from the secular world into a new life of ascetic training. A temple teacher shaves the head of a newly arrived apprentice.

329 » The scene of asura running amok.

Asurajang 아수라장

A chaotic scene. A rampage. Asura, a warlike demon in Buddhist lore who creates chaos, is often depicted as a monster with three heads and six arms. It is also shown with a half-male, half-female face. Buddhist paintings feature battlefields strewn with heaps of asura slain by Buddha's warriors. Despite their heavy losses, swarms of demons keep scaling the ramparts.

A mother who sees her boy's room littered with toys may say: "Your room looks as if asura has just torn it apart."

330 » Starving monster.

Akwi 아귀

Buddhists believe a greedy person becomes a "starving monster" after death. *Akwi* has "a stomach as large as a mountain but its mouth is as small as a needle's eye." So it's always starving. In Buddhist paintings, *akwi* looks emaciated and naked but has a protruding belly.

When people fight over food or bribes, Koreans call it *akwi datum*, or "starving monsters squabbling." A person eating voraciously is said to "eat like *akwi*."

331 » Geop.

Geop 겁

Imagine that you fill a castle with a 15-kilometer (9-mile) diameter with mustard seeds and let a bird fly in once every hundred years and take away one seed each time. How many years will it take for the castle to become empty? This virtually infinite length of time is called a "geop" in Buddhism. Monks say it takes 100 geops for an aspirant to become a Buddha.

Koreans say yuk geop, or "100 million geops," when they mean a very long period of time or "forever." The opposite concept of "geop" is "challa." Buddhists say that you can squeeze in 65 challas in the split-second it takes to snap your fingers.

"It all happened in a challa." It happened in a flash.

332 » Abi and Gyuhwan Hells.

Abigyuhwan 아비규환

Hellish scene full of blood and bodies. In 1995, a department store in Seoul collapsed, killing 501 people. It was one of South Korea's worst peacetime disasters and was blamed on shoddy construction. People called the scene "abigyuhwan," or the combination of two of many Buddhist hells, Abi and Gyuhwan.

"Abi Hell" houses those who killed their parents or Buddhist monks, damaged a Buddha statue or instigated a temple dispute. The condemned fall from a cliff into the gaping mouth of a black sea in a gale. The moment their bodies touch the sea, they disintegrate. The victims materialize on the tip of the cliff again and the ordeal repeats itself.

"Gyuhwan Hell" is for those who committed murder, thievery, adultery or drunken violence. They are skinned and thrown into flames or a boiling cauldron. They cannot crawl out because fierce guards are watching, and they never die and howl endlessly. Another description of this hell says those who suffered because of the condemned will appear as large serpents and torture them.

Jungyi gogimateul almyeon, jeole byeorukyi namji anneunda 중이 고기맛을 알면, 절에 벼룩이 남지 않는다

333 » When a Buddhist monk acquires a taste for meat, no flea will be left alive in his temple.

A meat-craving monk will settle for a diet of fleas. Most monks are vegetarians because their beliefs ban the killing of animals.

This saying warns against addiction and temptation. It also reflects prejudice against Buddhist monks during the Yi Dynasty. Monks were outcasts partly because they didn't marry, contravening the Confucian duty of every man to produce children to carry on the family lineage. The Yi Dynasty suppressed Buddhism, which had been respected by previous kingdoms.

Many monks retreated into valleys for meditation and scriptural study. Others stayed in towns, suffering persecution and risking "contamination" by the secular world while trying to propagate their religion. The first group was called *yipan*, and the latter *sapan*. Monks still debate which is the better path to follow.

When all options have run out and the situation is desperate, Koreans may say, *Yipansapanyida* – or "Neither *yipan* nor *sapan* worked."

Jukeun jung maejilhagi 죽은 중 매질하기

334》 ## Pummeling a dead monk.

As useless as criticizing a defeated enemy. Another expression dating from the Yi Dynasty era when the government persecuted Buddhists.

14 Proverbs as Propaganda

For decades, North Korea has used proverbs to encourage its people and denounce enemies.

Gaemiga jeongjanamu geondeurinda 개미가 정자나무 건드린다

335 » It's like ants trying to topple an oak tree.

An impossible task. In another context, the idiom hails the daring of the underdog. North Korea's state-run media prefer the latter definition when they cite the phrase in diatribes against the United States.

North and South Koreans share many expressions, which were coined well before their peninsula's division. Their punchy metaphors serve as a handy propaganda tool for the North. North Korean media cited an old proverb when Kim Jong Il became leader after the 1994 death of his father, Kim Il Sung, in communism's first hereditary transfer of power: "Streams know which gully to travel to reach the sea."

Official North Korea believed the transition of power to the younger Kim was as natural as streams flowing to the sea. The proverb reinforced the personality cult that Kim Jong Il inherited from his father. Its original meaning: Nature is evident in everything.

North Korea's government-issued dictionary defines proverbs as: "Concise and figurative language that describes experiences, lessons or social resistance that the working classes of people have accumulated through their lives and struggles over a long period of time."

The past decade has been the toughest time for North Korea since the Korean War. Floods and drought devastated its decrepit collective-farm industry. South Korean observers gleaned the following proverbs and expressions from North Korean dictionaries and recent publications. Many idioms extol tenacity.

- "When the bull butts you, he doesn't moo."
- "You watch your back when a dog that bites is around."
- "Even a deer will bite your leg if it gets angry."
- "You can tame a tiger, but you can't put a snare on a sparrow."
- "If our hearts are together, we can repel our hunger with one acorn."
- "You cannot buy hardship at a young age with gold." Hard work and sacrifice at a young age are priceless.
- "A tortoise picking a fight with the dragon."

A futile, self-destructive attempt. North Korea says the dragon is its People's Army, and the tortoise the United States.

When U.S. and South Korean forces launch joint military exercises, North Korea sometimes ridicules them as "moths flying into flame" or "fools rushing into flame with hay bundles on their back."

"As long as there is a rabid dog running around, the village is not safe." The rabid dog, North Korea says, is the United States. The saying exhorts North Koreans to be vigilant and loyal to the leadership.

Ppyeo eupneun hyeoga ppyeoreul busunda 뼈 없는 혀가 뼈를 부순다

336 » A boneless human tongue breaks bones.

North Korea is a master of tough talk, occasionally describing U.S. officials as "imperialist warmongers," "gangsters" and "ogres" even as it negotiates with them. In 1994, at the height of international tension over the North's suspected nuclear weapons program, a North Korean negotiator threatened to "turn Seoul into a sea of fire." When U.S. President George W. Bush called North Korea part of an "axis of evil," the North said Bush was a "puppy knowing no fear of the tiger." It dismissed comments by U.S. officials as "cock-and-bull stories."

Gaega jiteodo hangchaneunganda 개가 짖어도 행차는 간다

337 » The dog barks, but the caravan continues.

In North Korea's interpretation of this old proverb, the United States is an inconsequential mutt yapping at a mighty, surging caravan of revolution.

In a 1999 report, South Korea's National Intelligence Service quoted Kim Jong Il as saying: "We must ridicule the enemy with proverbs. Proverbs are a convenient national heritage when it comes to scoffing at the hostile classes."

North Korea has used the following expressions to denigrate its adversaries: "Even a dead cow would sit up and laugh until its muzzle is torn apart."

"It's so absurd that all the dogs of a village will run out and bark."

"That sounds like an autumn cuckoo."

There is no cuckoo in Korea in autumn, so the expression means nonsense or baseless rumors.

"However hard it tries, a crow can never become a pigeon."

A pet phrase in North Korea's criticisms of Japan.

"A dog tries to climb a willow tree."

You can try, but you will never succeed.

"You can't hide an awl in a cloth sack."

In this metaphor, the United States can't hide its "plot to stifle" North Korea because the conspiracy – the awl – will always stick out.

North Korean students and soldiers regularly hold seminars and debates and write theses on Kim Jong Il's aphorisms, which North Korean news media say "outshine those of Friedrich Engels and Vladimir Lenin in their depth and width." His government hails him as the nation's supreme language maven, who "explains everything in people's humble and easy-to-understand language, such as proverbs."

Kim's coinages: "If you are sincere, you can make a rock produce flowers."

"Live today: not for today's sake, but for tomorrow's sake." In 2001, North Korean shoe factory workers discussed this famous Kim remark. Their conclusion, according to North Korean media: workers should strive harder and produce more than planned.

“Let’s live according to our own way!” This political slogan, so popular that soldiers and students carry it in massive parades in Pyongyang, hails North Korea’s policy of *juche*, or self-reliance. The message is defiant, belying North Korea’s dependence on foreign food aid to feed many of its 22 million people.

Kim apparently inherited his knack for language from his father, who is credited with saying: “Capitalism is like weeds growing through the cracks of the pavement; wherever there is a hole, it raises its ugly head.”

More North Korean idioms:

- “Try to be a tomato rather than an apple.”

A tomato is red inside and out, an apt image for communists. The maxim means a man must match words with deeds.

- “The leaves fall, but the tree does not die.”

North Korea says its food shortages are passing difficulties like the falling leaves, and the nation will stand tall like the tree. It invoked this adage when the West wondered whether North Korea would be able to overcome deadly famine in the 1990s.

- “I’ve got everything except the cat’s horn.”

I’m as ready as I’ll ever be.

- “Looking at the sky through a bamboo pipe.”

Tunnel vision.

● "The toad jumps on the bean plant, looks around and admires how big the world is."

He is narrow-minded.

● "He would suck blood from a mosquito's leg."

He's brazen and ruthless.

● "There is no ugly man in fine clothes, and no handsome man in ugly clothes."

Take care with what you wear.

● "Going out to sell flour in a windy day."

A similar expression says, "It was windy when I went out to sell flour, and it rained when I went out to sell salt." A run of bad luck.

● "A bottle filled with water does not make noise."

A learned man doesn't talk much. The merit of taciturnity.

● "He is like a naked boy carrying a big general's sword."

He has his priorities mixed up.

● "The heaven gives the rain, and Buddha gets the bow."

● "It's like a dog seated on the throne of the dragon."

The man doesn't deserve his high post.

● "You look like a starving dog staring in the kitchen."

You look desperate.

● "She looked for a baby she was carrying on her back."

She didn't know what she was doing.

● "Kimchi is half your food."

Kimchi cabbage is the most important side dish in Korea. North Korean kimchi is less spicy and more watery than its

South Korean counterpart.

- "She sleeps with a chicken's neck as a pillow."

She is an early riser.

- "He fired artillery to kill a sparrow."

Much ado about nothing.

- "Like a mole digging a tunnel."

Describes a person who approaches a task with focus and perseverance. This phrase was in use long before North Korea began digging tunnels under the border with South Korea in the 1970s, allegedly for infiltration. After several tunnels were discovered, South Korea began comparing the North Koreans to "moles." A popular game machine in South Korea is called "Hunting Moles." From a dozen holes, plastic moles pop out randomly. The player thumps the moles with a mallet before they disappear into the holes. The moles used to have North Korean military hats.

- "He stuck to it like a lovelorn serpent."

He will never let it go. In folk tales, a man dies of love-sickness and turns into a large serpent that wraps itself tightly around a female victim. The woman lives with the serpent coiled around her body until a Buddhist monk or some other hero comes along to repel the snake.

- "He is trying to stack eggs on the bull's horn."

He is foolish.

- "He looks like a toad looking at a fly."

Eager, expectant.

● "You can't bite your own elbow."

There are things you can't do even if they involve you alone.

● "Even if it's a drought year, a snake doesn't eat millet."

No matter how dire the situation is, there are things you can't eat.

Haebangnyeo 해방녀

338 》 Liberated woman.

North Korean slang for a prostitute or an unwed mother. North Korea says there is no prostitution within its borders, but defectors from the country say otherwise. Prostitutes or unwed mothers suffer a greater stigma in the rigidly controlled North than in the South, according to North Korean defectors.

Michingaeneun mongdungyiga jegyeok 미친 개는 몽둥이가 제격

339 》 You should deal with a mad dog with a bat.

Be stern with adversaries. Some conservatives in South Korea say this when they fume at North Korea. Those hardliners remember when the North sent spies across the border, tunneled beneath it, dispatched submarines down the coast, tried in vain to assassinate the South Korean president in a commando raid in 1968, and allegedly engineered the 1997 bombing of a South Korean airliner in the skies near Myanmar, killing all 115 people on board. The North accused U.S.-backed South Korea of being a colony of the superpower. The South conducted its own propaganda campaign against the North, and officially ended infiltration efforts in the 1970s. Violence tapered off in the past decade as the South sought political reconciliation with the North.

Yubimuhwan 유비무환

340 » You won't have a crisis if you're prepared.

Be on your guard! This was the motto of South Korean leaders in the 1970s and 1980s who were determined to strengthen the military to guard against North Korea. Centuries ago, kings repeated the phrase in proclamations calling for a strong defense against Japanese invaders.

15 Behavioral Patterns

Swindlers, sweet-talkers, busybodies, and many others:
their manners are all captured in idioms.

Dotori kijaegi 도토리 키재기

341 » **Two acorns arguing which is the taller.**

That's like two spindly boys flexing muscles while a body-builder looks on.

Beondaegi apeseo jureum japneunda 번데기 앞에서 주름 잡는다

342 » **You are trying to show off your wrinkles to a silkworm.**

Quit boasting! You can't teach a fish how to swim. Koreans utter this put-down when a person tries to flaunt a skill in front of an expert. An example: a drunk slashing taekwondo chops before a black-belt master.

Mule ppajinnom guhaejuni bottari naenora handa 물에 빠진 놈 구해주니 보따리 내로라 한다

343 » **When I saved him from drowning, he criticized me for not saving his baggage as well.**

What an ingrate.

Son andaego ko pullyeo handa 손 안 대고 코 풀려 한다

344 » **He wants to blow his nose without using his own hands.**

He wants a free ride. A Korean mother puts a handkerchief or even her bare hand on her child's snotty nose. At the same time, she pretends to blow her own nose, snorting so that the child will do the same.

Da doen bape jae ppurigi/Da doen bape ko pulgi 다 된 밥에 재 뿌리기 / 다 된 밥에 코 풀기

345 》 She threw ashes (or blew her nose) into rice that's almost done.

Ruining a project on the verge of completion. Such provocative behavior litters the "Story of Nol-boo," a Yi Dynasty novel. Nol-boo is the most greedy, perverse and heartless character in Korean literature. An organ filled with vice protruded from under his left rib cage.

These are some of his favorite activities: Dancing at a villager's funeral; killing a dog when a village woman gives birth to a child (killing an animal is taboo during the sacred time of birth); forcing excrement into the mouth of a crying baby; fanning a neighbor's house in flames; taking the wife of a debtor who cannot pay his loans; grabbing the nape of an elderly man; relieving himself in a village well; poking holes in rice paddies to drain water and ruin the rice crop; driving a stake through a neighbor's green pumpkins; stomping on the back of a humpback; pushing down a man squatting to relieve himself so that he sits in his own excrement; kicking the chin of a disabled man; wielding a stick at a pottery dealer; stealing bones from graves; breaking a wedding engagement by spreading malicious rumors about the betrothed; scuttling a ship in high seas; punching a boil on a man's face; sprinkling pepper powder in the eyes of the innocent; slapping the cheek of a man with a toothache; sabotaging a deal in the marketplace; opening the lid of a neighbor's bean sauce jar while it's raining.

Nol-boo was rich but miserly. He wrote "Apple," "Meat" and "Rice" on pieces of paper and placed them, instead of real food offerings, on the table for ancestral rites.

Nol-boo's younger brother, Hung-boo, was poor but good-natured. One day, Hung-boo found a swallow with a broken leg. He cared for the bird and in late summer, the bird flew south with its family. When spring came, the swallow returned and dropped a gourd seed to Hung-boo. The poor man, who could barely feed his family, planted the seed and soon his thatched roof was covered with vines and enormous gourds. In the autumn, Hung-boo plucked the gourds, which were so large that he and his wife split them open with a large saw. Out burst jewelry and gold trinkets.

Nol-boo's special organ, *simsulbo* ("a bag of perverseness"), began to ache. The envious man caught a swallow, broke a leg and tied it with splints. The bird flew to the south and returned the following year with a gourd seed. But out of Nol-boo's gourds emerged monsters that kicked his buttocks, yanked his beard and sapped his wealth. One gourd spewed excrement on him.

Today, *simsulbo* means "a perverse person."

Hatbaji banggwi sedeut 핫바지 방귀 세듯

346》 He disappeared like a fart through a hemp pajama.

Not an elegant exit. *Hatbaji* – the coarsely woven, loose and drafty hemp pajama – used to be the standard garb for Korean commoners in summertime. The wealthy wore cotton or silk.

People in central Choongchung province are known for their decorum and distinctive drawl. Kings and scribes compared Choongchung people to *chungpungmyeongweol*, or "clean air and bright moon." People from other provinces considered them tenderhearted and weak, calling them *hatbaji.* Today, *hatbaji* refers to a meek, indecisive person, or a pushover.

"Do you think I'm *hatbaji*?" I will show you how tough I am.

Cheonyeoga aereul naahdo hal malyi itda 처녀가 애를 낳아도 할 말이 있다

347》 Even when a virgin gives birth to a baby, she has something to say to defend herself.

An outrageous excuse.

Dwieseo hobakssi kkanda 뒤에서 호박씨 깐다

348 》 She's peeling a pumpkin seed behind her back.

She's up to something fishy. An old tale explains the origin: A poor scholar studied all day, neglecting farm and household affairs. One day, he returned home to find his malnourished wife hurriedly concealing something behind her back. She wouldn't tell him what it was. After a quarrel, the distraught wife yielded a pumpkin seed. She was so famished that she had been peeling the seed to eat it. Ashamed of himself, the scholar studied ever harder to pass a government examination and secured a job at the royal court.

Over the years, the expression evolved from a commentary on hardship to a criticism of deceitful conduct.

Doduknom gae kkujitneun kkol 도둑놈 개 꾸짖는 꼴

349 》 He spoke like a thief chastising a dog.

A sheepish mumbler, trapped in an awkward situation. A similar expression: "He looks like a thief bitten by a dog." He has to be stealthy, and must hide the pain.

Byorukdo natjjakyi itda 벼룩도 낯짝이 있다

350 》 Even a tick has a face.

A potent insult. Say this about people who ask for too much, outstay their welcome, or try to get away with something.

Or "Even a weasel has a face."

Such a character is also called *chulmyeonpi*, or "one who's got a steel plate for a face."

If a person is humiliated, people say: "His face shrank to the size of a tick's."

Horangyiga yeolheuleul tteuteo meokeodo nameul saram 호랑이가 열흘을 뜯어 먹어도 남을 사람

351 » A tiger could maul him for ten days, but there would still be something left of him.

He's tough.

jongloeseo ppyam matgo hangangeseo nun heulginda 종로에서 뺨 맞고 한강에서 눈 흘긴다

352 » Get slapped in Chongno and look askance at people on the Han River.

Go home and kick the dog. Chongno is one of the oldest streets in downtown Seoul. It is several blocks north of the Han River, which bisects the capital.

Sonbadakeuro haneul garigi 손바닥으로 하늘 가리기

353 » You can't block the heaven with your hands.

Don't hide the obvious. In 1987, police tortured to death student activist Park Chong-chul, and denied it at first. In a comment that became a symbol of government abuse at the time, a senior police officer said: "They (police interrogators) just pounded on the table, but he doubled over and died."

South Koreans, outraged by the military government's attempt to "block the heaven with its hands," took to the streets. Four police officers were later convicted of killing the student while torturing him in a bathtub. Massive demonstrations forced the government of President Chun Doo-hwan to agree to democratic reforms, including more freedom of the press and a popular presidential election.

Chun, a former major general, seized power in a coup in 1979. A year later, Chun sent in paratroopers and tanks into the southern city of Gwangju when citizens rose up to oppose his military junta. When troops opened fire, the "citizens' army" armed itself with rifles from looted police stations and occupied the provincial government building. In an ensuing crackdown, hundreds of protesters died.

Later in 1980, Chun was elected president by thousands of pro-government delegates who gathered at a Seoul gymnasium to cast their ballots almost unanimously in his favor. Opponents mockingly called it a "gymnasium vote."

Mogi bogo kaleul ppopda 모기 보고 칼을 뽑다

354 》 He drew his sword because of a mosquito.

Much ado about nothing.

Bal beotgo naseoda 발 벗고 나서다

355 » He took off his shoes and rolled up his pants.

This is the same as rolling up your sleeves and getting down to work. Korean farmers work in rice paddies filled with ankle-deep water. Two-thirds of South Korean families engaged in farming until the late 1960s.

Yeopguri jjilreo jeol batgi 옆구리 찔러 절 받기

356 » She bowed to me only when she was nudged in her side.

She wasn't sincere.

Mot meokneun gam, jjilreona bonda 못 먹는 감, 찔러나 본다

357 » Poking holes in persimmons that he cannot eat.

Calling it sour grapes. The persimmon is a popular fruit in South Korea. There are two ways to eat them. One is to harvest them early, when the fruit is orange and still hard. Villagers peel the persimmons, and hang them to dry like beads on a string or stick. The fruits shrivel and turn into dark brown jelly, with powdery sugar forming on their skin. It's called *gotgam*, a favorite among children in the winter.

Another way to eat persimmons is to let the fruits hang on the trees well into autumn until they turn red and soft. Plucking them from the tree requires a deft touch because they easily split open. Clumsy pickers end up poking holes in the fruits' tender flesh. People suck the sweet flesh and throw away the skins. But they always leave some persimmons on the trees, calling them "food for magpies." That practice stems from a belief that every harvest must be shared with other creatures of nature. When a family has a big party or has an ancestral rite, the wife takes a little morsel of food and throws it outside the house in an offering to nature.

During a lunch break, an old farmer is likely to hurl a bit of food or rice wine in the air, shouting "Ko-shee-reh!" – or "Mrs. Ko!" A popular theory says that the ritual spread after people in a village began offering food to console the spirit of a woman, Mrs. Ko, who died of starvation.

Gamnamu miteseo ip beolligo itda 감나무 밑에서 입 벌리고 있다

358 ›› **She lay down under the persimmon tree, waiting for the fruit to fall into her open mouth.**

Waiting for a windfall.

Namui jesae gam nara bae nara handa 남의 제사에 감 나라 배 나라 한다

359 ›› **She's saying where to put persimmons and pears at other people's ancestral rites.**

She is meddling. In Korea, ancestral rites are meticulously choreographed, with each food offering occupying a designated place on the ritual table. It's a family affair, and outsiders shouldn't get involved.

Sachonyi ttang samyeon bae apeuda 사촌이 땅 사면 배 아프다

360 》 You get a belly ache if a cousin buys a patch of real estate.

You get envious when good fortune falls on a person you know, even if it's a close relative.

Gaeseongnyeoja nampyeon bonaedeut handa 개성여자 남편 보내듯 한다

361 》 The restaurant owner treats her customers as Kesung women send off their husbands.

She treats her customers with disinterest. Kesung, an ancient city in what is now southwestern North Korea, used to be a trade hub. Ginseng, called *insam* in Korea, was a big business, and Kesung traders sometimes traveled into China. Their resigned wives were so accustomed to seeing off their husbands that the farewells were drained of emotion.

Namui dari geulneunda 남의 다리 긁는다

362 》 Scratching somebody else's leg while sleeping.

You try to help yourself, but end up benefiting others. This also refers to an act that misses the point, or a person who says something irrelevant.

In a deep sleep, you scratch the leg of somebody sleeping beside you, thinking the leg is yours. You scratch harder and harder because satisfaction eludes you.

jiga hamyeon Romancego namyi hamyeon Scandal 지가 하면 로맨스고 남이 하면 스캔들

363 » If he's involved, he calls it a romance; but if others are involved, he calls it a scandal.

South Korea's rival political parties accuse each other of such hypocrisy. They raise allegations against their rivals, but downplay similar charges leveled against them.

Ipsule chimdo an bareugo 입술에 침도 안 바르고

364 » She lied without even moistening her lips with spittle.

She lied without qualms.

Beongaetbule kong kuweomeukgi 번갯불에 콩 구워먹기

365 » He can roast his beans with the flash of lightning and eat them while the flash lasts.

He's fast. A more common meaning these days is that the man is hasty, and therefore not reliable.

A folk story tells of a man who saw a woman jumping off a

cliff in a suicide attempt. He ran home to get a scythe, cut bamboo and split and wove it into a large basket, then ran back to the bottom of the cliff in time to catch the woman with the basket. They married.

Ppalli ppalli 빨리 빨리

366 » Ppalli ppalli.

Hurry, hurry! Koreans say “ppalli ppalli” when they want others to speed up. The term now symbolizes Koreans’ penchant for rushing things.

A favorite order at restaurants is, “What’s the fastest food you serve here?” Language institutes advertise *sok sung* – or “fast-result” – courses. Many passengers jostle in the aisles of a plane, taking down luggage, impatient to get off, even though the plane is still taxiing after landing. Bus passengers get up and lurch to the doors before the vehicle stops. They rush because the driver is impatient to move on to the next stop.

Ppalli ppalli is a Korean term widely known among restaurant owners and tour guides in Southeast Asia, Guam and Saipan – popular destinations for South Korean tourists.

Sociologists attribute ppalli ppalli to the country’s rapid economic growth. South Korea was reduced to ashes during the Korean War, but built itself into one of the world’s largest economies.

Critics blame ppalli ppalli for traffic jams, corruption, bad manners, jerry-rigged infrastructure that collapses, sometimes with fatal consequences, and the reckless expansion by corporations on borrowed money that contributed to Asia's currency crisis in the late 1990s.

Some taxi drivers honk horns and yell at other cars that move slowly. South Korea has one of the world's highest traffic accident rates. A traffic poster says: "While you try to reach your destination five minutes sooner, you could be gone forever."

Corrupt businessmen use what they call "hurry-up" money, a cash bribe to get government officials and contractors to speed up permits, licenses and deals.

Today's young South Koreans are more relaxed and seem in less of a rush. But ppalli ppalli still prevails among some Koreans, who move "as if they were being chased by something," as Koreans say about themselves.

Koreans have not always been in a hurry. The ancient elite considered running below their dignity. Sociologists say Koreans began changing as they went through the chaos and hardships of Japan's colonial rule and the Korean War. The great rush began when Park Chung-hee, an authoritarian general who ruled for 18 years until his assassination in 1979, shepherded the nation into rapid industrialization. He emphasized getting things done quickly, rewarding companies that built roads, bridges and plants faster than scheduled.

Gonggidanchuk, or "shortening the construction period,"

used to be a proud motto among Korean builders. Now the phrase is associated with sloppy workmanship.

Naembi munhwa 냄비 문화

367 ›› Tin pan culture.

Ppalli ppalli made Koreans resilient in times of crisis. But they have a tendency to react to a problem impulsively and quickly forget about it – a trend Koreans self-deprecatingly call *naembi munhwa*, or "tin pan culture." Water in a tin pan boils and cools quickly.

When a corruption scandal breaks, the whole nation seems to yell and shout. Newspapers bark headlines and people bad-mouth the government or protest in the streets. The hostility is such that political leaders scurry to find scapegoats and sometimes heads roll even though there is no hard evidence to prove wrongdoing by those who lose their jobs.

The uproars usually don't last and are rarely followed by a cool-headed analysis of what went wrong. In time, the country goes back to business as usual. Until the next scandal.

Maeumeun kongbate itda 마음은 콩 밭에 있다

368 ›› Her mind is in a bean patch.

Her mind is elsewhere. This phrase originally referred to a wild pigeon that perched on a tree, dreaming of a bean patch.

Bindae japdaga chogasamgan taewunda 빈대 잡다가 초가삼간 태운다

369 » He burned his hut to kill fleas.

He couldn't control his emotions.

Meokgi silchiman gae jugido silta 먹기 싫지만 개 주기도 싫다

370 » You don't want to eat it, but you don't want to give it to your dog either.

A miser.

Keoreum chigo jange ganda 거름 치고 장에 간다

371 » He was carrying compost when he followed others to the market.

He lacks discipline, forgets his task and is too impressionable. The place for compost is the field.

Kkoturi japda 꼬투리 잡다

372 » Grab the bean pod.

Find a decisive clue, especially incriminating evidence. If you grab the bean pod, it's only a matter of time before you get the beans.

More commonly, this phrase describes someone who likes to find fault with others.

"She is always grabbing the bean pod" means she's always looking for a chance to criticize others.

Sichimi tteda 시치미 떼다

373 » Cut the tag off the falcon.

Feign innocence. Koreans no longer practice falconry, but the tradition lives on in this popular phrase. Falconers attached a small identification tag on the leg or tail feather of their hawks. The tag, made of cow horn, was called *sichimi*. When some falconers saw a good hawk, they cut off the tag and pretended the bird was theirs.

Sanjeonsujeon 산전수전

374 » I have done battles both on hills and on seas.

I know hardship. A career veteran says this. Also, "His bones hardened in this field." He has been in this field since his youth.

Byendeokyi juk kkeulneun deuthada 변덕이 죽 끓는 듯하다

375 » He's as capricious as boiling gruel.

He changes his mind as often and randomly as bubbles pop up in boiling gruel.

Geolreuma nal salryeora 걸음아 날 살려라

376 » I begged my legs to save my life.

I ran as fast as I could. Some men and women also say, "I ran until I thought my crotch might split."

Usually out of earshot of women, men say, "I ran until my two balls clanged like bells."

Dalmyeon samkigo sseumyeon batneunda 달면 삼키고 쓰면 뱉는다

377 » She swallows what tastes sweet, and spits out what tastes bitter.

She only does what suits her.

Gwisin ssinarak kkameokneun sori 귀신 씨나락 까먹는 소리

378 » She sounds like a ghost threshing rice seeds.

She's talking gibberish. It's anyone's guess what a ghost sounds like when it's threshing rice seeds.

Oke ti 옥에 티

379 » A scratch on the jade.

A fly in the ointment.

380 » Horse station rumors.

Hamapyeong 하마평

Rumors or speculation about job reshuffles. Old government officials traveled on horseback, and their servants waited in "horse stations" while their masters did business in the palace. The lackeys exchanged gossip, which often concerned prospects for their masters winning a promotion. Today, when a government reshuffle is expected, newspapers carry *hama-pyeong* columns about possible candidates.

381 » Put an ink dot.

Nakjeom 낙점

Select a person for a job. In old Korea, aides to the king often provided him with a list of three candidates for a government post, and the king picked up his brush pen and put a dot before the name he wanted.

16

WISDOM

Many proverbs praise patience,
humility and hard work.
Parents and managers love them.

Bin surega yoranhada 빈 수레가 요란하다

382 》 **The empty cart makes more noise.**

For centuries, Koreans have applauded taciturnity and frowned on chatterboxes. "A man's word should be worth as much as a thousand kilograms of gold," they say.

Some Korean men take it too far. A common joke among housewives: "My husband says only three sentences when he comes home from work: Where are the kids? Give me something to eat. Let's go to bed."

Kaleul ppobateumyeon sseokeun hobakyirado chilreoya handa 칼을 뽑았으면 썩은 호박이라도 찔러야 한다

383 》 **If a man draws his sword, he should stab a rotten pumpkin at the very least.**

Actions speak louder than words. The phrase is timely when someone boasts of abilities but hesitates when the time comes to act. If a man wants to date a woman but balks at asking her out at the last minute, his friends taunt: "If you have your sword out, you must use it."

Gaettongdo yake sseuryeomyeon eupda 개똥도 약에 쓰려면 없다

384 》 **Even dog excrement is hard to find when you want to use it as medicine.**

A run-of-the-mill item is scarce just when you need it. The worth of a thing is best realized by the want of it.

Old people remember using dog excrement as medicine. When it was heated on a spade, a yellow liquid oozed out. Patients sipped the liquid mixed with water as a treatment for smallpox and other diseases, which swept through many villages.

People often supped children's urine to treat fevers, and some believed malaria could be cured by ingesting human excrement. Sometimes, a relative led the sufferer around the village, shouting "Buy malaria!" The aim of the symbolic gesture was to "sell" the malaria, forcing the disease's evil spirit to flee the victim's body.

When epidemics hit, stricken families summoned shamans or prayed to their many gods. They hung *geumjul*, or an "off-limits rope," across their house gates. Green pine branches dangled on the straw rope. A victim's family also sprayed red dirt around the house to warn other villagers to stay clear because the disease was in residence.

Soeppuldo dangime ppaera 쇠뿔도 단김에 빼라

385 》 If you intend to cut the bull's horn, you should do it in one stroke.

Otherwise, the bull will gore or trample you. The wisdom of swift, decisive action.

En bale ohjumnugi 언 발에 오줌 누기

386 » Urinating on frozen feet.

You'll warm your feet this way, but soon the urine will cool and turn to ice. A stopgap measure that aggravates the situation.

Ttongyi museoweoseo pihana, deoreoweseo pihaji 똥이 무서워서 피하냐, 더러워서 피하지

387 » You walk around a heap of excrement not because you fear it, but because it's dirty.

Shun bad people as you would filth. The phrase can also be used by people who avoid coming to grips with an awkward situation.

Hwajangsil galttae maum, olttae maum dareuda 화장실 갈 때 마음, 올 때 마음 다르다

388 » The person you are when you go to the toilet is completely different from the person you are when you walk out of the toilet.

Once on shore, we pray no more.

TOILET

In old Korea, the toilet was an outhouse: two parallel, wooden boards straddling a pit surrounded by mud walls below a thatched roof. A night visit to the backhouse was a precarious enterprise. Leaves and rice stalks served as toilet paper, and the modern stuff only became widespread in the 1970s. In South Korea today, it's just as likely to be found on a restaurant table as in the bathroom. Rolls of toilet paper serve as napkins.

In the outhouse days, people cleared their throats before entering. That gave surly spirits, believed to reside in the pit, time to take flight. If they lingered, the spirits were liable to trip you, pitching you through the hole and into the muck. The throat-clearing was also a practical means of knocking on the door. A person inside responded with the same noise.

On the southern island of Jeju, farmers let pigs wallow in the slime beneath the outhouse hole and gulp excrement as it flopped onto their faces. The island's pigs rarely feed on excrement today, but are still called "shit pigs" and their pork is considered a delicacy.

Farmers built the outhouse distant from the house for hygiene. They used buckets of waste as fertilizer.

Goteun namuga dokki meonjeo matneunda 곧은 나무가 도끼 먼저 맞는다

389 » The upright tree gets the axe first.

The intransigent will fall. Or the good die young.

Gineun nom wie ttwineun nom itgo, ttwineun nom wie naneun nom itda 기는 놈 위에 뛰는 놈 있고, 뛰는 놈 위에 나는 놈 있다

390 » If there's a creature that crawls, there's a creature that runs. If there's a creature that runs, there's always a creature that flies.

There's always someone better than you. This saying advises humility. It also refers to a scenario in which one villain outwits another. If a stooge is arrested for taking a payoff and the boss is found to have collected bigger bribes, Koreans say, "There's always a creature flying over a creature that runs."

Byeoneun ikeulsurok gogaereul sukinda 벼는 익을수록 고개를 숙인다

391 » As it ripens, the rice bows its head.

Wisdom and humility go hand in hand. The ear of a rice stalk droops with weight as it ripens. The tree branch that bears the most fruit hangs lowest, just as a humble sage avoids the limelight.

A similar saying: "Fish flock to deep water." A leader must have a good reputation and moral depth to attract a big following.

But Koreans also say: "If the water is too clear, fish won't gather." Try to be honest, but don't overdo it.

Nuweoseo chipbatgi 누워서 침 뱉기

392 » He's spitting into the sky while lying on his back.

He's shooting himself in the foot. The spit will rain down on his own face. The phrase often refers to a person who maligns close friends and relatives. The vitriol says more about the speaker than the accused.

Utneun eolgule chim mot baetneunda 웃는 얼굴에 침 못 뱉는다

393 » You cannot spit on a smiling face.

A smile softens your most ardent critics. In traditional Korea, people considered it virtuous to be strict and stern. Koreans still teach their children the Confucian values of respect for elders and superiors, and when to speak and smile. A person who smiles or laughs often in a family or office setting risks being branded as flippant.

Koreans have loosened up in recent decades. To be more competitive, businesses urge employees to be upbeat. Sales clerks practice smiling at training courses. "Whiskey, whiskey, whiskey," they chant, pulling their lips into a grin.

In Korea, people don't say "cheese" when they take photographs. They say "kimchi."

Sagongyi maneumyeon baega saneuro ganda 사공이 많으면 배가 산으로 간다

394 » **If you have too many ferrymen on a boat, it sails up the mountain.**

Too many cooks spoil the broth.

Seom jigo bule ttwieodeunda 섬 지고 불에 뛰어든다

395 » **It's like walking into fire with a bundle of straw on your back frame.**

Like digging your own grave. Many farmers still use a wooden back frame called *jige*, or "shoulder device." Some of the first Westerners to come to Korea called the device an "A-frame" because it is shaped like the letter A. The frame was good for carrying everything from rice sacks to sick grandparents to a drum of excrement for compost.

Bal eopneun malyi cheolri ganda 발 없는 말이 천리 간다

396 » **Even without legs, words can travel 1,000 miles.**

Rumors, especially malicious ones, travel far and fast. Watch what you say. The saying is a pun in Korean because *mal* means both "word" and "horse."

Sam bate ssukdae 삼 밭에 쑥대

397 » If mugwort grows among hemp stalks, it grows tall.

One surrounded by excellence will inherit the quality. If dwarfed by its plant neighbors, mugwort grows taller than usual to reach for the sun.

Baneul doduk so doduk doenda 바늘 도둑 소 도둑 된다

398 » A boy who steals a needle grows up to steal a cow.

If you start out rotten, you'll only get worse. The cow was the most coveted family possession in Korea, a predominantly agrarian country until the early 1970s. A cow thief was the worst kind of robber.

As the country industrialized, poor farmers saw education as a way to propel their children out of the drudgery of a life tending the rice paddies. Some sold their cows to send their kids to college. Many workers in Seoul's high-rises reminisce about their parents' sacrifices. The most common expression of their gratitude: "My dad sold his cow to send me to college."

Garangbie ot jeotneun jul moreunda 가랑비에 옷 젖는 줄 모른다

399 In a drizzle, you don't realize you are getting wet.

Minor setbacks lead to downfall.

Bae bateseo got kkeun gochiji mara 배 밭에서 갓 끈 고치지 마라

400 Don't touch your 'got' (hat) in the pear orchard.

Don't arouse suspicion. Reach for that hat, and you might be accused of reaching for the branches to steal pears. *Got* is a tall, black Korean hat with a wide, flat brim, made of horsetail hair. In old Korea, married men of high social status wore this hat when they traveled. Today, virtually the only people who wear it are actors and singers in traditional arts performances.

Also: "Don't tie your shoes in a melon field."

Cheon gil mul sokeun alahdo han gil yeoja sokeun moreunda 천 길 물 속은 알아도 한 길 여자 속은 모른다

401 You may know what's in 1,000 fathoms of water, but you will never figure out a one-fathom woman.

Women are a mystery.

Sodo eondeokyi iteoya bibinda 소도 언덕이 있어야 비빈다

402 A cow needs a slope to rub its back.

A friend in need is a friend indeed. The lonely say, "I don't have a wall to rub my back."

Mateun nomyi dari ppeotgo janda 맞은 놈이 다리 뻗고 잔다

403 》 **The man who did the beating sleeps with his legs pulled up to his chest; the man who was beaten sleeps with his legs stretched out.**

You'll never feel at ease if you do something bad. The assailant has more to worry about than the victim.

Cheoumen saramyi suleul masijiman, najungen sulyi sarameul masinda 처음엔 사람이 술을 마시지만, 나중엔 술이 사람을 마신다

404 》 **In the beginning, man drinks wine. But in the end, wine drinks man.**

Drinking destroys.

Ssoteun ssaleun damado baeteun maleun mot damneunda 쏟은 쌀은 담아도 뱉은 말은 못 담는다

405 》 **You can retrieve spilled rice, but you can't take back words that left your mouth.**

Think twice before you speak. A fable: A royal court minister saw a farmer tilling his field with two cows, one yellow and one red. The minister asked the farmer which cow was stronger, but got no reply. The official asked again but the farmer kept working in silence. The minister fumed and shouted.

Finally, the farmer approached him and whispered: "Sir, I think the yellow cow is stronger. But I couldn't answer you aloud because the red cow would hear and be disappointed."

The minister learned a lesson that day.

Ah dareugo, uh dareuda 아 다르고, 어 다르다

406 ## There is a big difference between 'Ah' and 'Uh.'

Watch your words. Be attentive to nuances.

Gaman iteumyeon jungganeun handa 가만 있으면 중간은 한다

407 ## If you sit still (keep your mouth shut) now, you might at least finish the game in the middle of the pack.

Sit tight and things will turn out OK. A person who rashly tries to say or do more than expected deserves to hear this barbed remark. Seniors say it to youths or subordinates who don't hesitate to make their opinions known.

Sanawun gae kotdeung seonghannal eopda 사나운 개 콧등 성한 날 없다

408 ## A quarrelsome dog's nose has no time to heal.

This describes a person or organization that is always embroiled in strife.

Homiro makeul geol garaero makneunda 호미로 막을 걸 가래로 막는다

409 》 **If you hold off filling the hole in your rice paddy with a hoe, you may end up using a spade.**

A stitch in time saves nine. The rice paddy is usually filled with ankle-deep water, and farmers take exceptional care to prevent water leaking out.

Kong simeunde kongnago, pat simeunde patnanda 콩 심은 데 콩 나고, 팥 심은 데 팥 난다

410 》 **If you sow yellow beans, you get yellow beans. If you sow red beans, you get red beans.**

You reap what you sow.

Maedo meonjeo matneun geotyi natda 매도 먼저 맞는 것이 낫다

411 》 **If you have to get caned, it's best to get it over and done with first.**

Bite the bullet. The sooner, the better. Caning was a common method of disciplining schoolchildren and punishing criminals. Schoolteachers used hickories. For criminals, the type of rod and the number of lashes depended on their transgressions.

A thief was often tattooed on his forehead or arms with "Thief" or "Robber." Such a punishment was called "kyong."

Gyeongel chil nom – or "He deserves the 'Gyeong' punishment" – is a common curse today.

Jeolmeoseo gosaengeun saseodo handa 젊어서 고생은 사서도 한다

412 » You should welcome hardship at a young age, even if you have to buy it.

Elderly people who endured the Korean War and the decades of poverty that followed say this to youths to remind them of the value of sacrifice. Young Koreans heard this a lot until the 1980s, when affluence began to chip away at the old wisdom.

Han umuleul para 한 우물을 파라

413 » When you are digging a well, keep digging in one place.

Be consistent. People who worked at the same job for their whole career say proudly: "All my life, I dug one well." Koreans also say, "You can't chase two rabbits at the same time."

Koreans took lifetime employment at one company for granted during the country's boom years in the 1980s and early 1990s. They were shocked when businesses began laying off workers during the 1997-98 Asian currency crisis, and workers held violent protests. In the old days, people who switched companies for more pay or a higher post were often seen as opportunistic and disloyal. No longer.

Namwi jangdane chumchunda 남의 장단에 춤춘다

414 》 Stop dancing to another man's tune.

Mind your own business. A middle-aged man pulled out all his black hair to win admission to the chess game played by old villagers. Later, he pulled out his white hair to mix with younger people playing poker. He ended up bald.

Jiseongyimyeon gamcheonyida 지성이면 감천이다

415 》 Heaven will be impressed if you are very sincere and industrious.

Heaven helps those who help themselves. One of the most common proverbs that parents hammer into the heads of their children. Talent isn't that important. No matter how impossible a goal looks, Koreans believe hard work and perseverance will make things happen. Parents set lofty goals. Ask grade-school boys about their future, and many say, "I want to be President," or "I want to be a great General."

Today, high schools and villages hang large banners of congratulations when a hometown boy passes make-or-break exams to become a lawyer or government official. The family throws a party for the whole village. A 'Korean Bill Gates' is a common label attached to a successful young businessman.

Daldo chamyeon giunda 달도 차면 기운다

416 When the moon is full, it begins to wane.

Success is fleeting. So be humble even at the peak of your powers. "No power lasts more than ten years," Koreans say as a warning to the powerful. In ancient royal courts, coups and plots were rampant and many kings and court ministers failed to last ten years.

Two authoritarian presidents were in office more than a decade. Founding President Syngman Rhee was in power for 12 years until pro-democracy demonstrators forced him to fly into exile in Hawaii in 1960. Park Chung-hee took power after Rhee and ruled for 18 years until he was assassinated by his own intelligence chief in 1979. In democratic South Korea, the president serves a single five-year term and cannot seek re-election.

Horangyineun jukeumyeon gajukeul namgigo sarameun jukeumyeon yireumeul namginda 호랑이는 죽으면 가죽을 남기고 사람은 죽으면 이름을 남긴다

417 When a tiger dies, it leaves its fur. When a man dies, he leaves his name.

Man must build a good reputation.

SOURCES

Most of the expressions in this book were gleaned from personal memory, contemporary Korean publications and everyday talk. The following sources were also consulted:

- 『The Encyclopedia of Korean Culture』, The Academy of Korean Studies, Seoul, 1991.
- 『Collection of Korean Oral Literature』, The Academy of Korean Studies, Seoul, 1980-86.
- 『Doosan Encyclopedia』, Doosan Corp., Seoul, 2000.
- 『A Dictionary of Korean Proverbs』, Lee Ki-moon, Ilchogak, Seoul, 1980.
- 『A Dictionary of the Korean Language』, Lee Hee-seung, Minjungseorim, Seoul, 1986.
- 『A Collection of Common North Korean Terms』, National Intelligence Service, Seoul, 2000.
- 『A Collection of 400 North Korean Terms』, Yonhap News Agency, Seoul, 1999.
- 『A New History of Korea』, Lee Ki-baik, Ilchogak, Seoul, 1984.
- 『Yipansapan, Yadanbeopseok: Understanding Buddhist Terms』, Ahn Kil-mo, Bulgwang, Seoul, 1993.

- Proverbtopia: http://hometopia.com/proverb/indexpro.html
- Proverbs: http://twinpapa.com.ne.kr/

How Koreans Talk

Published by Unhengnamu
4th FL. Namsung Bldg, 385-15 Seokyo-dong, Mapo-gu, Seoul, Korea
Tel : 82-2-3143-0651 / E-mail : ehbook@chollian.net

First print May 20, 2002
Sixth print Sept. 23, 2005

ISBN 89-87976-95-5 03740